FIRE
ISLAND
LIGHTHOUSE

FIRE ISLAND LIGHTHOUSE

. . . .

LONG ISLAND'S WELCOMING BEACON

BILL BLEYER

THE
History
PRESS

Published by The History Press
Charleston, SC
www.historypress.net

Front cover: Lighthouse, keeper's quarters and lens building. *Copyright 2016 Audrey C. Tiernan*.
Back cover, top left: The spiral staircase. *Copyright 2016 Audrey C. Tiernan; center*: Unidentified
early keeper. *Courtesy Fire Island National Seashore; right*: The lighthouse's first-order Fresnel
lens displayed on the site. *Copyright 2016 Audrey C. Tiernan; bottom*: The lighthouse at sunset.
Copyright 2016 Audrey C. Tiernan.

First published 2017

Manufactured in the United States

ISBN 9781625859778

Library of Congress Control Number applied for.

Notice: The information in this book is true and complete to the best of our knowledge. It is
offered without guarantee on the part of the author or The History Press. The author and
The History Press disclaim all liability in connection with the use of this book.

CONTENTS

ACKNOWLEDGEMENTS

Bob LaRosa and Dave Griese of the Fire Island Lighthouse Preservation Society for initiating the project and Patti Stanton and Bette Berman of the society for providing research help and historic photos.

For help with research, historic photographs and graphics: lighthouse historian Robert Müller, MaryLaura Lamont of Fire Island National Seashore, Steve Harrington, Tim Harrison of *Lighthouse Digest*, Jeff Gales and Thomas Tag of the U.S. Lighthouse Society, Jo-Ann Carhart of the East Islip Public Library, Captain Dan Berg, Jim Claflin of Lighthouseantiques. net, Geoff Karlin and artist Frank Litter.

Audrey C. Tiernan for the stunning photographs of the light station in its current glory.

For help with processing the photographs: Elizabeth DeMaria and Susan Sarna of Sagamore Hill National Historic Site.

My diligent proofreaders/fact-checkers: Joe Catalano, Dave Griese, Harrison Hunt, Bob LaRosa, Susan Sarna and especially Natalie Naylor.

My supportive editors at The History Press: J. Banks Smither and Abigail Fleming.

And to Joe Catalano for overall support throughout the project.

INTRODUCTION

The Fire Island Lighthouse was built to warn mariners approaching a barrier island of the sandbar that could fatally entrap their vessels. But the tower also served a contrasting—and unplanned—mission: it functioned as a welcoming beacon for millions of immigrants coming to America in the late nineteenth and early twentieth centuries. It provided a first glimpse of their new homeland.

The 1858 lighthouse also became a local landmark and lasting point of pride for Long Island mariners and other residents. Including me. As a native Long Islander who has spent his entire life boating, I am a longtime admirer of the Fire Island Lighthouse. As a resident of the North Shore, I didn't have much exposure to it until the 1980s, when I began going on scuba diving trips out of nearby Captree State Park through Fire Island Inlet to the ocean. Viewing the beacon from a distance, I was—and remain—entranced by its graceful curves erupting majestically from the sandy landscape of the barrier island like a rocket poised for launch. Soon after that, I visited the site and was awestruck by the setting, the view from the tower and how the structures allowed me to transport myself back into the maritime past. I returned to the lighthouse in the 1990s to write the first of many articles about it for the Long Island daily newspaper *Newsday* and nautical magazines.

For those who live closer to the lighthouse, especially residents of Fire Island, it remains an important local icon. As a 1983 National Park Service report pointed out:

The Fire Island Light is not only the most visible structure on Fire Island, it is also the oldest. It is therefore an appropriate symbol for the historical evolution of the barrier island and of a local economy whose more representative structures—beach houses, small craft, boatyards, and docks—have usually been short-lived. The Light Station has also become the symbol of the natural evolution of the area, as its initial placement at the original western tip of Fire Island is the most graphic example of barrier beach dynamics.

The 1981 nomination form for inclusion of the site in the National Register of Historic Places offered additional testimony to the property's significance on the thirty-two-mile barrier island: "Fire Island Light Station also served important non-navigational functions in the nineteenth century, with the keeper and his assistant serving as 'mayors' of Fire Island, assisting baymen, and serving as inn-keepers to rich urbanites seeking primitive recreation experiences away from the city."[1]

For the New York City metropolitan area, the National Park Service report states, the lighthouse complex is important for its role in helping the

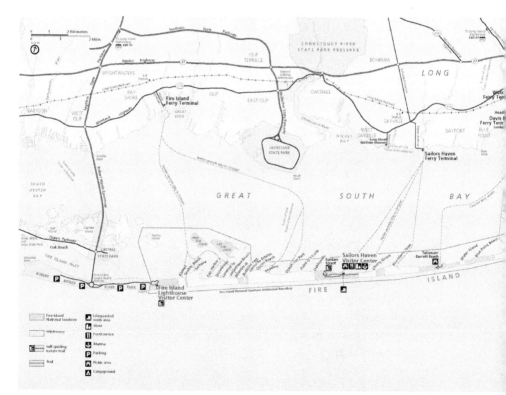

city become the predominant trading center in the United States in the late nineteenth century. "New York's emergence as the most important American port in the transatlantic trade made the Fire Island Light the most important light on the East Coast," the report noted.

And on the national level,

> *the Fire Island Light Station serves as a symbolic structure illustrating the evolution of national involvement in public works, interstate and foreign commerce and coastal defense. These national themes might be illustrated at other sites in other locations; but in this area, the Fire Island Light is the salient structure. The light itself was also the first landfall for ships approaching New York from Europe, and so it was usually the first American structure seen by the millions of immigrants who entered during the peak years of immigration between 1880 and 1910. The architectural merit of the light station is high. Exceptionally well-designed, it has a graceful curved profile and was built with a number of attractive architectural details.*[2]

Courtesy of the National Park Service.

The lighthouse and entrance sign from the Fire Island access road. *Copyright 2016 Audrey C. Tiernan.*

The importance of the lighthouse as an aid to navigation diminished in the second half of the twentieth century. It was eclipsed by radar and Global Positioning System technology, making the idea of peering through the fog for a flashing light atop a tower a quaint throwback to a more romantic, but dangerous, era. Yet while the light and tower became less important for high-seas commerce, they remained an important visual reference for the local boating community.

That was not enough reason, however, for the Coast Guard to continue to staff and pay ever-increasing maintenance costs to keep the lighthouse functioning. So in 1973, the beacon was extinguished and replaced with a modern lamp apparatus atop the nearby Robert Moses State Park water tower to the west. The Coast Guard personnel were transferred and the structures left to deteriorate. Paint peeled, and the concrete coating began to flake off the tower

Local boaters and residents feared that despite its history and symbolic importance, the lighthouse might face demolition like its counterpart at Shinnecock to the east had in 1948. But a dedicated group of volunteers formed a nonprofit organization, the Fire Island Lighthouse Preservation Society, and partnered with the National Park Service to save the structures from oblivion. The society and the agency went on to restore them and even managed to have the tower relit in May 1986 after a dozen years of darkness.

So today, those traveling the Atlantic Ocean and the Great South Bay or enjoying the beaches of Long Island's South Shore can still marvel at the view of the lighthouse. While it still serves a navigational purpose, the beacon now is primarily a year-round tourist attraction. Most visitors—those not coming from Kismet or other Fire Island communities to the east—follow the Robert Moses Causeway from West Islip across the bay to the barrier island. They park in the lot at Robert Moses State Park Field 5 and then walk three-quarters of a mile on a boardwalk through sand dunes and low-lying wind-twisted vegetation to the light station. About 173,000 visitors a year, including 6,000 schoolchildren, make the trip to soak up the site's salty past and view the free exhibits in the keeper's quarters, boathouse and lens building erected to house the original first-order Fresnel lens, which returned to the site in 2011. Approximately 32,000 of them—who meet the requirement of being at least forty-two inches tall to safely navigate 180 spiral and straight steps—pay a fee to climb the tower. With the assistance of a Dacron rope that replaces the earlier hemp running from ring to ring on the outer wall, they huff their way up to the outdoor gallery ringing the tower just below the lantern. From there, they are rewarded with stunning 360-degree views of the ocean, the bay, the South Shore of Long Island, the communities to the east and the state park and causeway bridges to the west. On extremely clear days, the views can include the Manhattan skyline,

An aerial-view postcard before the boathouse was moved closer to the bay and replaced by the lens building. *Author's collection.*

View of the Manhattan skyline from the top of the tower. *Courtesy of Bette Berman.*

about forty miles away. When they descend, those who made it to the top receive a free certificate attesting to their climbing feat.

The public is not allowed access to the narrow ten-step ladder leading to the lantern room. Those privileged to climb that high get an even better view from the tall windows. But they need to be careful to avoid being struck by the aero-beacon light; its back-to-back one-thousand-watt bulbs rotate counterclockwise day and night to create a flash every seven and a half seconds visible from twenty-one to twenty-four miles. Looking at the bulbs would result in serious eye damage, and even being in their proximity negates the need for a coat in winter.

From the tower to the boathouse to the lens building, "the Fire Island Light Station is a fine example of preserving and interpreting the maritime heritage of Long Island and America," said Dave Griese, who retired as chief park ranger at Fire Island National Seashore in 2001 and became executive director of the Fire Island Lighthouse Preservation Society.

But the lighthouse that people visit today is not the first one erected on Fire Island. The current tower, built in 1858, replaced a shorter and impractical one constructed in 1826.

This book recounts the story of both lighthouses. It tells of the shipwrecks that proved the need for the beacons and the lightships that augmented them in the late 1800s and early 1900s. And it details how the current lighthouse was saved and the future plans by the Fire Island Lighthouse Preservation Society to augment the visitor experience.

1

THE NEED FOR A LIGHTHOUSE

A Dutch brig, *Prins Maurits*, was the first recorded shipwreck off Fire Island, in 1657. Hundreds more would follow in the succeeding three centuries.

Prins Maurits and its crew of 16 was transporting 113 colonists from Amsterdam to Delaware on a voyage that began on Christmas Day 1656. After a rough passage with storms blowing away sails, the crew sighted land on March 6, believing it to be Manhattan Island. But since no one aboard was familiar with the region, the ship crept toward shore, with sailors frequently checking the depth with a weighted line. When the water began to get shallow, the crew tried to reverse course but was unsuccessful. About 11:00 p.m., the bow plowed into the sandbar that runs the length of the South Shore about a quarter mile offshore. At dawn, those aboard saw they were mired just off a barren beach. A leaky lifeboat was lowered and in numerous trips got everyone to shore near today's Saltaire without any casualties. Tents were made from sails and spars. But there was no driftwood to make fires. The survivors were discovered on March 12 by Native Americans, 2 of whom agreed to carry a message to New York governor Peter Stuyvesant in Manhattan. The day after learning of the wreck, he dispatched a small sloop to aid the group on the beach. Nine other ships followed from New Amsterdam to aid in the recovery, which was accomplished after the Native Americans showed them Fire Island Inlet. In April, the colonists finally made it to their intended destination, what is now New Castle, Delaware.[3]

Postcard view of the lighthouse. *Author's collection.*

As trade and immigration from Europe boosted the number of vessels in and out of the port of New York, there was a commensurate increase in the number of vessels that ran afoul of the sandbars parallel to the barrier islands. The low-lying beaches that separated the Atlantic Ocean from the bays along Long Island's South Shore had few houses or other structures to give warning to mariners traveling on dark nights or through fog. If they did not hear the breakers running up on the beach on a rough night, their first indication of trouble would be their keels grinding to a halt in the sand. It did not help that the offshore sandbars were constantly shifting. Fire Island and the other barrier islands were constantly stretching westward, as the littoral drift, or prevailing current, shifted sand down the shoreline. Once trapped on the sandbars, extrication was usually difficult, if not impossible. The remains of ships and their cargoes were salvaged by the few Fire Island inhabitants, South Shore residents who crossed the Great South Bay or "wreckmasters" appointed by local officials to oversee the disposition of the doomed vessels.

Congress recognized the danger for mariners and the need to do something on the national level. It passed legislation on August 7, 1789, stipulating that all expenses for building and maintaining lighthouses and other aids to navigation would be paid by the federal treasury. To deal with the hazards of the waters off Long Island, President George Washington approved the establishment of a lighthouse at Montauk Point at its eastern tip in 1795 after New York State provided the land. The eighty-foot octagonal tower was completed in 1797 at a cost of $22,300.

The Montauk Light could help mariners find the end of Long Island. But the most direct Great Circle Route, followed by vessels headed from Europe to New York, bypassed Montauk for landfall farther west. Until the first Fire

The *Savannah*, depicted in a 1944 U.S. postage stamp, was the first ship to use steam power on a transatlantic voyage. It ran aground and broke up off Moriches near the eastern end of Fire Island in 1821. *Photo by the author.*

Postcard view of the lighthouse. *Author's collection.*

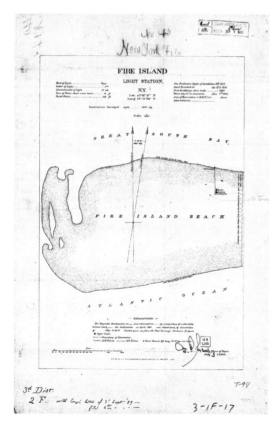

Map of the west end of Fire Island in 1825. *Courtesy of the National Archives and Records Administration.*

Island Lighthouse was constructed in 1826 and the Shinnecock Lighthouse farther east in 1857, there was no guide for ships between Montauk and New York, a distance of almost 120 miles. That proved to be too far on many occasions. One of them was November 5, 1821, when the *Savannah*, bound from that Georgia city to New York, wrecked off Fire Island.

The 120-foot vessel launched in New York on August 22, 1818, had been designed as a transatlantic sailing packet. But it was also equipped with a one-cylinder ninety-horsepower steam engine. The vessel gained notoriety in 1819 when on a voyage from its namesake city to Liverpool it was propelled by steam alone for eighteen days of the trip—the first use of steam power on a transatlantic voyage. By the time *Savannah* approached Long Island in 1821, the engine had been removed. When the ship ran ashore and broke up off Moriches near the eastern end of Fire Island, Captain John Coles of Glen Cove and the ten other men aboard perished. The *New York Daily Advertiser* reported that Coles's trunk washed up on the beach and was broken open by the waves, spilling gold and silver coins among the victims. The sole witness, Smith Muncy, turned over all of the money he found to a wreckmaster. Another disaster occurred on Christmas Day 1824, when the French vessel *Nestor*, carrying a cargo of dry goods, ran aground off Fire Island and was destroyed.[4]

The need for a lighthouse between Montauk and New York City grew with the opening of the Erie Canal in 1824. With New York now the entryway to the Great Lakes, the additional shipping traffic allowed the metropolis to eclipse Boston and Philadelphia as the major port of the nation.[5]

Because of wrecks like the *Savannah* and *Nestor* and the ever-increasing shipping to and from New York, ship owners lobbied aggressively for a lighthouse on Fire Island, where the inlet on the western end provided access into the Great South Bay and refuge from storms, at least for smaller vessels that could navigate a channel that was constantly filling up with sand. It wasn't until 1826 that they got their wish.

2

THE FIRST LIGHTHOUSE

I t took four years after the loss of the *Savannah* for Congress to act.

Finally convinced of the need for another aid to navigation between Montauk and New York City, the lawmakers on March 3, 1825, appropriated $10,000 to purchase sixty-four acres at the western tip of Fire Island for construction of a lighthouse. They followed up on April 20 by passing a bill giving the United States exclusive jurisdiction over land in Suffolk County for lighthouse purposes. But it was unclear who, if anyone, owned the property on the east side of the inlet. Jonathan Thompson, the federal superintendent of lighthouses, wrote on June 15, 1825, that he was unable to obtain title and requested that the state legislature cede jurisdiction over the tract. After it complied, Thompson arranged to have the land appraised. It was 2,112 feet from the low-tide mark on the ocean to the low-tide line on the bay and 1,320 feet from east to west. Tredwell Scudder, Smith Carll and Samuel S. Gardiner valued it at $50, which Thompson paid to the state. The title was issued on May 7, 1825.[6]

The federal government decided the tower would be located on the southwest corner of the property about 120 feet from the ocean. The design was one that had already been used in many early lighthouses, including Montauk Point; Sandy Hook, New Jersey; and New London, Connecticut. Thompson notified potential contractors of the specifications for the structure in a run-on sentence of hundreds of words. It began:

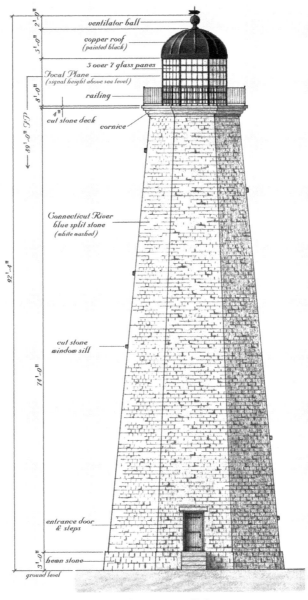

ventilator ball

copper roof
(painted black)

5 over 7 glass panes

Focal Plane
(signal height above sea level)

railing

4"
cut stone deck

cornice

Connecticut River
blue split stone
(white washed)

cut stone
window sill

entrance door
& steps

hewn stone

ground level

2'-0"

5'-0"

8'-0"

89'-0" FP

92'-4"

74'-0"

3'-0"

scale 1/8" = 1'-0"

Exterior Elevation
(south side)

Illustration of the 1826 lighthouse. *Courtesy of Steve Harrington.*

The Light House is to be an Octagonal Pyramid to be built of Connecticut River blue split stone and the best quick lime and sand mortar, the foundation wall to the 7 feet thick from the base to the water table, and tapered to two feet six inches at the top of the pyramid; the height of the building to be seventy-four feet above the water table to the bottom of the lantern, thirty-two feet diameter at the water table, and sixteen feet diameter at the top of the pyramid; the foundation to be layers of square timber, thirty-four feet in length, placed transversely, six feet below the surface.

Thompson went on at length in minuscule detail. He specified that "the floorings to be supported with strong sound timber, and floored with one and a half inch plank, grooved together....The top of the lantern is to be a dome five feet high, water tight, and covered with copper, thirty two ounces to the square foot...and the building to be well pointed with cement, and white washed twice over, inside and outside." (See the full, exhaustive specifications in Appendix C.)

Thompson specified that the lighthouse and adjacent keeper's dwelling must be completed by the end of December 1826. He said separate contracts would be awarded for equipping the lighthouse within a month after its completion "with eighteen patent lamps and plated Reflectors, highly burnished, and all the necessary apparatus to make the same complete; the lights to be fitted up on the most approved revolving plan" along with eight tin containers of eighty-gallon capacity for storing lamp oil. The lighthouse superintendent signed a contract with Haviland Wicks to construct the tower for $7,000. Another $1,200 contract was given to George W. Thompson for the lamps, reflectors and other equipment.[7]

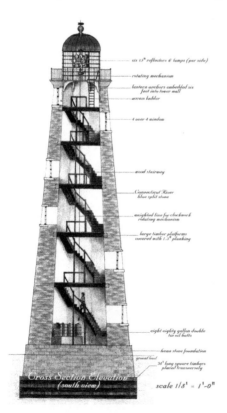

six 13" reflectors & lamps (per side)

rotating mechanism

lantern anchors embedded six feet into tower wall

access ladder

4 over 4 window

wood stairway

Connecticut River blue split stone

weighted line for clockwork rotating mechanism

large timber platforms covered with 1.5" planking

eight eighty gallon double tin oil butts

hewn stone foundation

ground level

34' long square timbers placed transversely

Cross Section Elevation (south view)

scale 1/8' = 1'-0"

Cutaway illustration of the 1826 lighthouse. *Courtesy of Steve Harrington.*

The tower, which had six windows and was painted white, was completed and illuminated in late 1826, but the exact date is unknown. The total cost was $9,999.65. The leftover $0.35 from the $10,000 allocation was recorded as "surplus funds." Despite Thompson's meticulous effort to spell out quality standards for the tower, the construction was problematic, as subsequent observers would document.[8]

The specifications called for the light to be located at 89 feet, 3 inches above sea level and be visible fourteen and a half nautical miles under "ordinary atmospheric conditions." But contemporary reports said the light was reported to be visible for twenty-seven nautical miles. Wayne Wheeler, founder of the United States Lighthouse Society, calculated that this would have been impossible. He determined that a mariner would have had to be at a height of 225 feet to see the light over the horizon from twenty-seven nautical miles away. In addition, the original lamp and reflector system did not generate enough light to be seen that far. Wheeler noted that the much more efficient first-order Fresnel lens in the subsequent lighthouse only had a range of about twenty-four miles. The eighteen lamps with 15-inch reflectors designed by Winslow Lewis were much criticized. They were mounted on a chandelier that rotated once every ninety seconds. This was accomplished by a weight attached to a cable that had to be cranked by hand to the top of the tower every four hours. A governor mechanism controlled the speed of the rotation. The lighthouse would emit a flash as each lamp and reflector aligned with an observer. But the problem of the dim light fixtures was compounded by the small panes of glass around the lantern room.[9]

The first keeper, who was not officially appointed until 1827, was a man named Isaacs; his first name does not appear in the records. He served until 1835. More than one hundred other keepers and assistants would follow at the two Fire Island light stations. Some would have long tenures, such as Seth R. Hubbard, who served as second assistant keeper, first assistant keeper and then keeper from 1873 to 1881. At the opposite end of the spectrum was assistant keeper Uriah Brown, who lasted only three weeks in the summer of 1870. The reason for his early departure is not recorded.

The keepers of the first lighthouse had to cope with problems stemming from its poor design and shoddy construction. Those shortcomings were documented in 1838 by U.S. Navy lieutenant William D. Porter during an inspection trip of lighthouses from New York to Virginia. Commenting on the Fire Island lighting apparatus—with its eighteen lamps with spherical reflectors mounted on three parallel rows—Porter wrote that the "reflectors

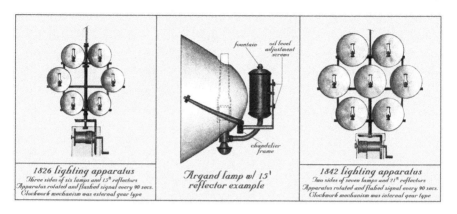

Illustration of lighting apparatus in the 1826 lighthouse. *Courtesy of Steve Harrington.*

are badly placed, and do not stand perpendicularly, but have an inclination of two or three degrees from the line of focus. The stone of which the tower is built, good; but the cement is bad, and crumbles; arch leaks....Lantern appears to be too small for the number of lamps; I therefore recommend that the lower tier be dispensed with. Sills of windows rotten." Porter singled out the Fire Island Lighthouse for criticism in his summary comments, comparing it unfavorably with a Delaware beacon: "The main tower erected on Cape Henlopen, years previous to the American Revolution, is at present strong and solid, without crack or flaw in the workmanship, and still exhibits evidence of continued durability; whereas the tower at Fire-island inlet, built apparently after the model of that at Henlopen, is of modern date, has undergone several repairs, and is yet leaky."

Inferior design and workmanship was the unfortunate hallmark of many lighthouses built during the reign of Stephen Pleasonton. The penny-pinching accountant with no technical background headed the United States Lighthouse Establishment, created in 1820 during James Monroe's presidency.[10]

At the time of Porter's visit, the keeper was Felix Dominy, appointed in 1835. He was an East Hampton clock and watchmaker from a family famous for making fine furniture. Porter's report included an excerpt from Dominy's "private note-book" that illustrates the ongoing need for maintenance and repairs as well as how difficult navigation along the coast could be in those early years, even with a lighthouse on Fire Island:

1836, June 21, brig Rhine *stranded. December 14, brig* General Trotter *came on shore; total loss. January 14, ship* Tamarac, *(English, from Liverpool,) assorted cargo, 120 passengers; cargo lost, first boat upset; passengers and crew landed in long-boat, with the assistance of people from shore. November 29, sloop* Report *on shore. August 21, white-washed the house; Captain Barker ten day's repairing the light-house. September 9, sloop* Traffic *on shore.*[11]

In a March 30, 1840 letter to his son Nathaniel—one of five children he raised with his wife, Phoebe Miller—Dominy described one shipwreck:

Yesterday a brig got on shore about a mile west; on the bar—from Palermo in Italy, Captain Nicolo Haggio, bound to N.Y. loaded with wine, oranges, Madeira nuts, almonds, figs, raisins, lemons, grapes, anchovies, capers, apricots, preserve, cherries, etc. etc. The men eleven in number all speak Italian & one of them speaks English rather broken but we can make out to understand him so he interprets for the whole. They seem to be quite a nice set of men altogether. They have over 300 boxes of oranges, lemons, sweet-oil & pickles they went ashore on West Beach & were pick'd up by some men from Babylon. I went over today in the fog and brot [sic] home 1 box oranges & one of lemons the crew brot onshore figs & nuts....It has been so foggy they have not been able to board the brig since they first left her but we are in hopes of getting on board in the morning and getting out the chronometer, sailors dunnage, and a few boxes of silks and silk velvet belonging to the Captain. They seem very clever and liberal telling us to get as many nuts, oranges, lemons, wine etc. as we want.

Dominy's letter goes on to recount a minor accident in the tower that could have been much more serious:

One night I went up in the lt. house to trim the lamp & walking back wards fell down the trap door until my right foot reach'd the stairs & thought at first my leg was broken crawled up & laid down on the floor for a while & got partly over it & hobbled down. Tis about 10 days & I have got pretty much over it my knee is a little stiff it was so lame for 2 days I was obliged to use a cane & once in a while it made me fairly hallow out loud now I can run quite spry.

Dominy also wrote about supplementing the menu at the lighthouse by shooting waterfowl. "I have killed but few birds this spring—got 21 duck one day," he noted.[12]

Many of the early lighthouse keepers worked at other trades simultaneously to supplement their income. In his time at the lighthouse, Dominy developed a lucrative sideline in the hospitality trade. He became a successful innkeeper on Fire Island and on the other side of the bay in Bay Shore. Those extracurricular activities resulted in censure by district lighthouse superintendent Edward Curtis. He wrote in 1843 that Dominy "entertains boarders and company at his dwelling in the Island and devotes so much of his time and care to that, and other business personal to himself that the public charge committed to him, is not fully exercised; his Light House duties are made subordinate objects of attention." Curtis also complained that Dominy had allowed the lamp reflectors recently installed at the lighthouse to be damaged by his neglect. He also accused Dominy of providing alcoholic beverages to his guests. As a result, Dominy was discharged.[13]

Nothing was done in the immediate wake of criticisms of the lighthouse leveled by Porter and other observers. But with continued complaints from

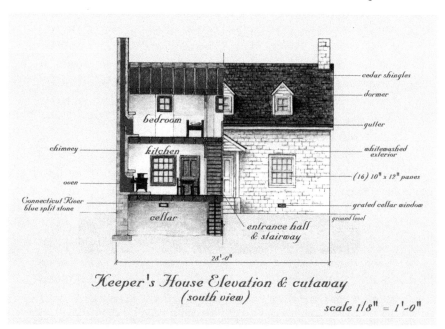

Cutaway view of the keeper's quarters at the 1826 lighthouse. *Courtesy of Steve Harrington.*

mariners, in 1842, the lantern was refitted with fourteen larger lamps with twenty-one-inch reflectors. This was reported to provide a light with a range of twenty-two miles, but that is highly questionable, as observers complained the illumination was hardly improved.

Eliphalet Smith replaced Dominy as keeper on January 15, 1844. Eleven days later, he was visited by a cousin from Illinois, Elizabeth Howell Blanchard, a native Long Islander born in Baiting Hollow in 1800. Despite, or because of, poor health, she decided to travel home in 1844. In a June 26 diary entry she talks about a "large party" going to Fire Island, where they arrived "at Capt Smiths, found them finely situated. Had a fine dinner....We rested awhile then proposed to go up to the top of the Light-house. It is seven stories high. Quite a curiosity to see the apparatus up there, the large silver reflectors which cost forty dollars apiece. They are splendid. Then to look abroad on the vast ocean and think of the dangers of the great deep and turn and look the other side and see a broad expanse of water calld [sic] the bay. With numerous crafts of all sizes almost and pursuing as many occupations."

Her entry the following day noted that her cousins were "paid by the government five hundred dollars for lighting and tending the light house and they do live very finely indeed." On the third day she wrote again about spending time at the top of the lighthouse:

Took my pen and ink and assended [sic] *the 7 flights of stairs and am comfortably seated in the top of the light house on Fire Island, a grand oppty to contemplate the majesty and power of him who can say to the winds and waves, "Peace be still." The sun shines glorious and the wind blows tremendous. The surf and surge, roar and beat upon the shore. A true touch of the sublime is this view of the mighty ocean, constantly pouring in roaring and foaming its white billows against the sandy beach. None but an omnipotent arm could save a frail barque of a ship from the ravages of the great deep. I do not, cannot see how tis possible for man to presume to sail out upon the wonderful expanse of water without imploring divine protection from the dangers of the sea!*

Blanchard returned home to Illinois, where she died two years later.[14]

Selah Strong was appointed keeper on July 14, 1849, succeeding John A. Hicks. Strong, who would serve four years, was visited on June 12, 1850, by a supply ship commanded by a Captain Howland. The captain reported that the tower had undergone recent repairs such as whitewashing and re-pointing "where the cement was off and loose." The lantern was being upgraded with larger windows. Howland wrote that repairs were needed on the dwelling, including fixing the well, installing a new oven, painting and constructing a fence. He did say that, contrary to other reports, the lighting apparatus appeared to be "in good order and clean."[15]

The public clamor for an improved aid to navigation at Fire Island dramatically increased in volume in 1850 with the wreck of the barque *Elizabeth* and the death of a famous passenger: women's rights advocate, Transcendentalist and journalist Margaret Fuller. The five-hundred-ton ship had sailed from Livorno, Italy, in mid-May, bound for New York City with a $200,000 cargo that included oil paintings, silks, almonds and a marble statue of former vice president and secretary of state John C. Calhoun. Seven days out, as the ship was about to leave the Mediterranean, the captain died of smallpox, and first mate Henry Bangs assumed command. He was far off course when he sighted the Fire Island Light and confused it with the beacon at Cape May, New Jersey, in a July gale. About 3:30 a.m., *Elizabeth* drove onto a sandbar three hundred yards from the beach and about three miles from the lighthouse near Point O' Woods, New York. The impact ejected passengers from their bunks. The next wave lifted the stern and pushed the ship broadside to the breakers. That caused the cargo of marble to shift and the statue of Calhoun to be propelled through the side of the hull, allowing it to flood.

As the ship began to disintegrate under the assault of breaking waves, all of its lifeboats were smashed or washed away. After two sailors successfully used planks to reach the beach, passenger Horace Sumner tried to replicate their feat but quickly sank. The rest of those on board decided to wait for help. A crowd gathered, but the spectators were more intent on salvage than helping those stranded on the *Elizabeth*. A volunteer lifeboat crew based near the lighthouse did learn of the ship's predicament and prepared to help, but with no immediate indication of aid from the beach and the tide starting to rise, the officers urged the passengers to make for shore on planks rigged with ropes and pushed by sailors. The volunteer surfmen arrived but did not launch their boat into the heavy surf. After two more hours of no useful activity by the would-be rescuers, the acting captain urged everyone to "Save yourselves!" and jumped overboard. Most of the crew followed. Fuller, however, could not swim, so she; her husband, Giovanni Ossoli, an Italian marquis; their infant son; and four sailors remained onboard. Finally, more than ten hours after the grounding, the ship began to break up. The remaining mast toppled, and a mountainous wave broke over the hull and carried the seven holdouts away. Seven of the twenty-one on *Elizabeth* died.

About $15,000 worth of silk was carried off by the crowd, and six people were arrested later for theft. Writer Henry David Thoreau came to Fire Island to search for Fuller's remains, but he was unsuccessful. A pavilion with a memorial plaque to Fuller was erected in Point O' Woods in 1901, but it was destroyed in a storm in 1913. The statue of Calhoun was later salvaged from seven feet of water at low tide and installed at the capitol building in Columbia, South Carolina, where it remained until it was destroyed when General William T. Sherman's Union troops arrived in the closing days of the Civil War in 1865.[16]

Writer Margaret Fuller, whose death in 1850 created momentum for building a new Fire Island lighthouse. *Library of Congress*.

The loss of the *Elizabeth* and Fuller's death made international headlines. She had been a writer for the *New York Tribune*, whose influential editor, Horace Greeley, wrote her obituary. "America has produced no woman who in mental endowments and acquirements has surpassed Margaret Fuller," he said. Poet Ralph Waldo Emerson wrote that "it is a time that the United States, instead of keeping troops and forts, should keep a coast guard of lighthouses to defend lives and property."[17]

The still mostly unmitigated hazards of sailing along the South Shore were described by Nathaniel S. Prime in his 1845 *History of Long Island*:

> *In the whole length of the island there are but ten openings in the Great Beach and these are constantly varying, by the violence of the waves, so that after a single storm, the channel, which is never deep, may be materially obstructed or changed. This necessarily renders the coasting business on the whole south side exceedingly uncertain and precarious; at the same time accounts for these awful disasters which have so often been attended with the most appalling consequences on this ill-fated shore. From Coney Island to Montauk Point, there is not the vestige of a harbor that can be entered by a sea-vessel. If, therefore, by mistake of reckoning, or other cause, a ship is brought near the coast, with a strong bearing on shore, or a breeze too light to beat off, her doom is usually sealed.*[18]

The outcry over the *Elizabeth* helped drive the movement to build taller lighthouses. The result was that nine brick towers more than 150 feet high would be built at Fire Island and eight other sites along the eastern coastline by the end of the decade. But in the interim, there were problems with the rotation mechanism and illuminating apparatus of the Fire Island Light in the 1850s. Apparently, a new illuminating apparatus was installed in 1854, with more repairs two years later. But the overall problems with the light station remained as long as the first tower did.[19]

3

THE U.S. LIFE-SAVING SERVICE

The first lifesaving operation on Fire Island was a group of volunteers operating out of a garage.

In 1847, realizing that lighthouses alone were not going to prevent all shipwrecks, Congress took action to improve the chances of survival for victims of maritime disasters. It appropriated $5,000, supplemented by an additional $10,000 the following year, to establish volunteer lifesaving patrols on Long Island and New Jersey beaches.

The first lifesaving station built on Fire Island was a garage erected in 1849 to store a surfboat and other rescue equipment along with provisions for any shipwreck survivors who might seek refuge there near the lighthouse. It was supplemented by six other stations along Fire Island by 1854.

Even with sometimes spotty coverage, the part-time volunteer "surfmen" saved many lives. But there were still large gaps in the safety net for distressed mariners. As a result, the volunteers were replaced by full-time paid surfmen at some stations in New Jersey as an experiment in 1870. In 1871, based on those results and in acknowledgement that the volunteer system was inadequate, Congress allocated $200,000 for the secretary of the treasury "to employ crews of experienced surfmen at such stations and for such periods as he might deem necessary and proper."

With those funds, a station resembling a house was built just west of the lighthouse in 1872, and wings were added five years later. In 1920, it was replaced by a third station.

A crew conducts a drill on August 31, 1908, at the second U.S. Life-Saving Service station built near the Fire Island Lighthouse. *Image from the Vagts Collection of the Suffolk County Historical Society Library Archives. Copyright © Suffolk County Historical Society. All rights reserved.*

The first keeper appointed to run the lifesaving station, in 1850, was Selah Strong, who was also the lighthouse keeper. Later that year, Benjamin Smith took over; in 1853, he became the lighthouse keeper and served in that role until 1861. In 1872, Warren Clock, who was also the lighthouse keeper, served for a year as lifesaving station keeper. He was replaced by Edmund Brown, who was only there in 1873. Leander Jeffrey or Jeffries was the station keeper from 1875 to 1880 followed by Charles E. Wicks from 1885 to 1900, John T. Doxsee from 1901 to 1913 and finally Harry F. Smith from 1913 to 1914. The following year, the U.S. Life-Saving Service was merged into the newly formed U.S. Coast Guard.

In the early days, the only tool available to the surfmen was a heavy wooden surfboat that they could pull to the scene of a wreck on a wagon. Then they donned oilskins and cork lifejackets, launched through the surf and made multiple trips to the doomed vessel to retrieve passengers and crew. The surfboats were later augmented by "beach apparatus." This consisted of a small cannon called a Lyle Gun along with ropes, pulleys and wooden supports for the ropes. The gun shot a nineteen-pound steel projectile attached to a spool of rope out to a grounded ship, where the crew would attach it. The surfmen would then use the initial line to get a heavier rope called a hawser out to the ship and then attach a "breeches buoy" to bring crew and passengers ashore one at a time. Those being rescued would sit in the breeches (an oversized pair of canvas shorts) attached by pulleys to the line over their heads and then be pulled over—but sometimes through—the waves to the beach by the surfmen. In later years, the breeches buoy was replaced in some locations by a "surf-car," also known as a life-car, invented by Captain Douglas Ottinger of the U.S. Revenue Cutter Service. These sealable metal capsules—with the victims inside to protect them from the elements—would be pulled back and forth between a stricken ship and the beach on a hawser like the breeches buoy. An original Fire Island surf-car is on display in the boathouse of the lighthouse museum complex.

The beach apparatus, while unwieldy, was highly successful. Between 1871 and 1915, it was used to rescue more than seven thousand people from 720 vessels off Fire Island.[20]

4

BUILDING THE SECOND TOWER

T he Fire Island Lighthouse was already obsolete when it was placed into service in 1826. And by the time it entered its third decade of operation, it was clear to everyone except the federal official in charge of lighthouses that it needed to be replaced.

Like other early coastal lights, the Fire Island tower was too short to be seen far enough out to sea to be effective. That problem was compounded by its poor design and shoddy workmanship, faults that were exacerbated by deterioration caused by the harsh weather. The result was that ships continued to wreck off the barrier island. The issue was not addressed because of how the federal government managed the aids to navigation. The lighthouses were under the control of a Treasury Department official with the odd title of "fifth auditor" from 1820 until 1852. Stephen Pleasonton not only lacked maritime and engineering experience but also had many other unrelated duties diverting his attention.[21]

Most experts agreed the premier lenses available were those fabricated from designs by the brilliant French engineer Augustin Fresnel (1788–1827). He recognized that the existing system with the light from lamps concentrated and directed by reflectors was inherently inefficient. Even with the best possible mirror, half the light would be reflected and the other half absorbed. And no mirror was perfect; the surfaces were never totally reflective, getting the angle of the parabolic curves right was difficult and cutting a hole in the reflector for the lamp's burner interfered with focusing the light. Fresnel realized the solution was to replace the reflectors

East elevation drawing of the 1858 lighthouse. *Courtesy of Fire Island National Seashore.*

with a lens. The lens, by refraction, or bending of light, could take all the light emanating from a lamp and focus it into a beam just like mirrors did by reflection. But instead of losing half of the light generated, a lens would only lose about one-twentieth of the illumination. The engineer also realized that using a single traditional-style lens would require the apparatus to be gigantic. Fresnel solved this problem by dividing the lens into concentric circles, with each prism bending the light from the source into one parallel line. The system was called dioptric, or based on refraction. Fresnel completed his prototype in 1820, and the inventor devised a classification system with six sizes of lenses. The largest, first-order major coastal lenses, had an interior diameter of six and a half feet. To help mariners distinguish one lighthouse from another, Fresnel proposed three types of lights: fixed, or continuous, and two rotating devices, one that flashed every thirty seconds and another once a minute.[22]

Fresnel's brilliant innovation made lighthouses many times brighter and more economical. By the 1850s, Fresnel lenses had been installed throughout Europe, Africa, Asia, South America and around the Caribbean. But even as the American merchant fleet became the world's largest and American ports thrived in the early part of the nineteenth century, the United States refused to abandon the old reflector system. The primary obstacle to implementing the new technology was Pleasonton. The miserly accountant could not see why he should pay $5,000 for a lens when a traditional reflecting illumination apparatus cost less than $1,000. Pleasonton was convinced that the U.S. lighthouse system already was the best in the world, as well as the most cost-efficient.

It required intervention by Congress before the United States even tested a Fresnel lens. In 1838, the lawmakers directed the U.S. Navy to evaluate the efficiency of different illumination systems. When the service recommended testing the Fresnel lens against the reflecting system, Congress arranged it over Pleasonton's objections. Captain Matthew C. Perry, who in 1854 would force Japan to open its doors to foreign trade, was directed to acquire two Fresnel lenses: a first-order fixed one and a second-order revolving type from France. Pleasonton tried to sabotage the test by refusing to pay for the lenses, even though Congress had already appropriated the funds. Eventually, the Henry Lepaute Company of France was paid, and the lenses shipped to New York in March 1840. The test was conducted at the Navesink Highlands light station in New Jersey. Despite Pleasonton arguing that using the Fresnel lenses would require hiring skilled engineers to serve as keepers and greatly increase costs, the tests were considered a success—but not by Pleasonton, who called the $18,975 cost for the two lenses and their installation extravagant and refused to buy any more. That generated more complaints from maritime interests. In 1842, eighty-two merchant captains petitioned for "a thorough examination by competent and disinterested persons." Dozens of insurance underwriters from New York and Boston made the same demand. Congress responded by appointing civil engineer Isaiah William Penn Lewis to examine lighthouses in Maine and Massachusetts. After his

An early painting of the second lighthouse that hangs in the keeper's quarters museum. *Courtesy of the Fire Island Lighthouse Preservation Society.*

tour, Lewis condemned the existing system, but Pleasonton was steadfast. Lewis ultimately prevailed by persuading Congress to have the Corps of Topographical Engineers rather than the Lighthouse Establishment build five East Coast lighthouses equipped with Fresnel lenses in difficult sites. Sankaty Head on Nantucket Island in Massachusetts was the first one lit, on February 1, 1850, with a second-order Fresnel lens from Lepaute. It became the brightest lighthouse in New England, visible from the mainland forty-one miles away.[23]

With complaints about the poor lighthouses increasing, the government sent a commission to Europe to examine how the beacons were managed there. The information gleaned persuaded Congress to professionalize lighthouse management. In March 1851, it instructed U.S. Treasury secretary Thomas Corwin to create a temporary United States Light-House Board consisting of two navy officers, two army engineers and a civilian scientist. The initial appointees favored reform. After fog delayed several members of Congress on a steamship off Sandy Hook, New Jersey, because the lighthouse reflector lighting system was so dim, on October 9, 1852, the lawmakers placed all of the nation's lighthouses under the jurisdiction of a new, permanent and independent U.S. Light-House Board. It retained the original members of the temporary board and added a second civilian scientist, Joseph Henry, first director of the Smithsonian Institution. The legislation divided the country into twelve districts, and an inspector was assigned to each. The inspectors—initially all naval officers—quickly became overworked, and an engineer was appointed for each district. The board ordered that all new lighthouses be equipped with Fresnel lenses. And it stated that one of its goals was to make travel into New York "easy and safe," to facilitate the city becoming the most important American port in transatlantic trade. That meant Fire Island would become the most important

SHINNECOCK LIGHT HOUSE, HAMPTON BAYS, L. I., N. Y.

Shinnecock Lighthouse, from which a lens was moved to Fire Island in 1933. Built in 1858, the deactivated lighthouse was demolished in 1948. *Author's collection.*

light station on the East Coast. And so in 1852, the board recommended raising the height of the tower and equipping it with "the most powerful lens apparatus that can be procured." But no action was taken immediately.[24]

The board decided first to add a new lighthouse on Long Island's South Shore to fill the long gap between Fire Island and Montauk before dealing with Fire Island. It built the Great West Bay Lighthouse, more commonly known as the Shinnecock Lighthouse, at Ponquogue in Good Ground, which was renamed Hampton Bays in 1922. The new tower was lit on January 1, 1858.

The Fire Island upgrade was made possible when on March 3, 1857, Congress appropriated $40,000 for a 168-foot tower. The specifications called for it—as with Shinnecock—to be equipped with a huge first-order Fresnel lens that would be visible for at least twenty-one miles. Commander Thorton A. Jenkins, secretary of the lighthouse board, notified the U.S. Army Corps of Engineers officer who would be in charge of the project, Lieutenant J.C. Duane, of the appropriation in a letter on March 24, 1857. He said the first-order revolving lens apparatus should cost about $10,000, leaving $30,000 for the tower. He added that the focal point of the light should be at least 150 feet above mean low water. Jenkins instructed Duane to give "early attention" to the project because of its importance.

The original specifications cannot be located. But the second tower was constructed 200 feet northeast of the original lighthouse on a stone pier 100 feet by 150 feet. The brick structure has walls almost 11 feet thick at the base and tapers to 2.5 at the top. There are nine landings. The design of the tower is unique in New York State. A lamp with multiple wicks was placed inside the first-order Fresnel lens, which was mounted inside a lantern, or glass enclosure, 11 feet, 4 inches wide with glass 9 feet, 9 inches high.[25]

An illustration of the 1858 tower. *Courtesy of Steve Harrington.*

Construction presented complications, as seen in letters from Duane to the lighthouse board secretary. On April 8, 1857, he expressed concern about building the tower to the desired 168-foot height with the materials specified: "Even if brick were to be employed this material does not appear to me to be adapted to a work of such importance in such an exposed situation. I would, therefore, recommend that stone be used in this case. The present appropriation would be sufficient to build the tower and probably the lantern, leading the apparatus to be purchased from a new appropriation or some other source." The engineer officer's recommendation was ignored, presumably because of the higher cost of stone. So Duane provided an estimate dated June 1, 1857, that itemized the $32,345 cost of building the lighthouse out of brick. It included $8,000 for 800,000 bricks, $1,500 for 1,200 pounds of cement and $4,000 for 1,610 days of work by masons.

On June 3, 1857, the board informed Duane that his estimate was approved, with one exception: a system of iron ties proposed by the engineer to strengthen the brick structure. He was authorized to proceed with construction as soon as the money was available, which would be July 1. The preparation of plans and ordering of materials was documented in the lighthouse board's 1857 annual report: "The wharf, store-house, and temporary barracks for the accommodation of the workmen have been constructed, and the greater part of the material required for the construction of the tower has been procured and landed at the site, and it is expected that the tower will be completed and ready for exhibiting the first order lens from it by the middle of the next summer."[26]

William Lane was hired as construction overseer. He arrived on June 22, 1857, and hired a pile-driver and crew to begin working on the foundation. There is no record of when construction actually began. Drawings prepared by Duane and dated June 2, 1857, show five courses of granite resting on and filled in with concrete, with the granite slabs laid radially in a cantilevered pattern. The foundation was not completed until the spring of 1858, as bad weather forced the project to shut down in December. When Lieutenant J.T. Morton, who had replaced Duane, arrived in the spring and inspected the foundation, he was not pleased. He explained in an April 9, 1858 letter to the lighthouse board that "it occurred to me to try with a pick, the concrete filling of the foundation, which had a bad appearance....It would be assuming a great risk to my reputation to build on a foundation that might prove unreliable." The engineer had a hole dug and found the concrete down to two and a half feet was "quite friable and porous; the mortar could be reduced into a powder between the fingers, easily." He surmised that too much water and sand had been added to the mix and frost had damaged the concrete while it was drying. He worried that the "weight of the tower would...occasion some settling in the mass which would crack and disfigure the tower, and there is a certain possibility that the tower might soon be ruined by some granite giving way of its bed." He proposed removing the bad concrete because "it will not cost much: the concrete can be sifted, and the broken stone be used again."

The board rejected Morton's suggestion on April 10. Two days later, he offered an alternative. He wanted to double the number of reinforcing iron bands proposed by Duane that would be embedded in the lower ten feet of the tower. He said they would "effectually prevent any spreading or cracking:

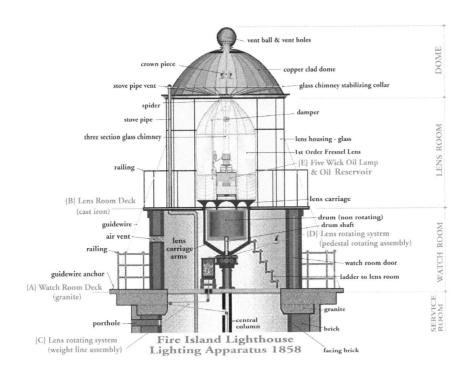

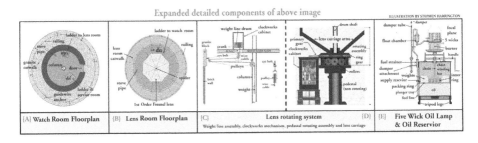

An illustration of the top of the 1858 tower. *Courtesy of Steve Harrington.*

the additional expense will be very little, the bands or anchors being made on the spot, and the additional strength will be very considerable." On April 14, the board accepted the alternative plan. Morton resolved the issue of the foundation's potential instability in an April 19 letter to the board: "I am glad to state that the concrete samples that I took from the F.I. foundation have become much firmer, and quite hard in fact, by being allowed to set in a warm room."[27]

As for the tower, the plans called for its wall to be constructed of three concentric rings. There would be a thin cylindrical inner wall extending up to the sixth landing, and the middle layer was to be twice as thick and cylindrical but not as tall. The outer one was to be concave, tapering inward as it rose to meet the middle ring. The concentric rings of brick were reinforced by eight radial brick walls with shafts between the rings to allow for drainage and ventilation. The board told Morton on May 27 that with the tower up about twenty feet above ground level and with brick no longer having to be cut to match the planned curves, he should be able to average about a foot a day in height going forward. It also informed Morton that the tower was to be painted yellow. In July, Morton began experimenting to find the best cement wash and color for the tower. He wrote to the board that two coats totaling one-eighth of an inch of cement should "render the tower impervious to water." He was still looking at different color possibilities to "find one which will give an agreeable cream yellow colour."[28]

Work continued on schedule during the early summer. But then, with money and materials depleted, Morton wrote to Captain William Franklin, the lighthouse board secretary, on August 16 with a recommendation:

> *Sir: I believe it is your intention to have the old Tower and Dwelling at Fire Island torn down on 1ˢᵗ November next.*
>
> *I have therefore proposed to tear down the stone part of the dwelling at once, in order to use the stone in building the foundation of the new Dwelling.*
>
> *The old Tower will furnish the stone for the superstructure of the new Dwelling, but it will of course not come in play this season.*
>
> *The light keepers can live in the workmen's shanty this winter and I will have it made perfectly tight and comfortable for them. The Oil Room shall be built next to the tower of brick, as there will be enough for that left; the oil room forms a part of the new Dwelling, but I can build it sufficiently to answer the purpose, with a temporary roof, during the winter.*
>
> *The above arrangement seems the best I can make, and there is but one objection to it.*
>
> *The present keeper is disinclined to live in the frame part of the house till he moves into the shanty. In this he is wrong, as the frame is comfortable enough except in winter; and when that comes he can move into a good tight shanty, nearly as convenient as his house.*

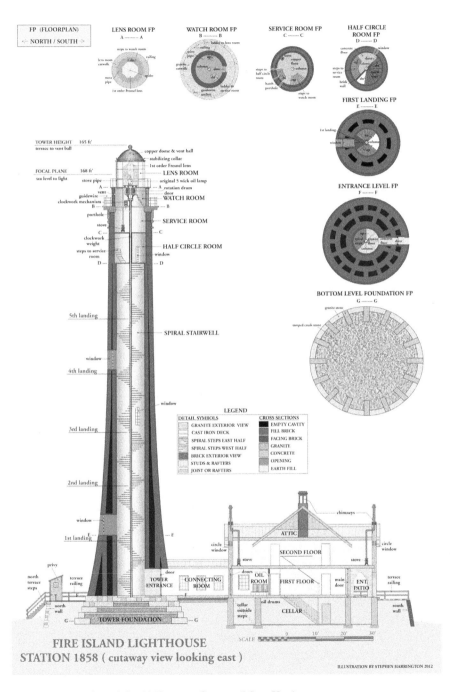

Cutaway illustration of the 1858 tower. *Courtesy of Steve Harrington.*

Should you approve of my arrangements, I would request that the keeper may have orders to move out of the stone part of his house at once.

The board responded to Morton's letter on August 16, ordering keeper Benjamin Smith to vacate the dwelling when Morton told him to do so. The board also informed the engineer that the keeper would require a second assistant for the new light station and that Morton should provide sufficient housing.[29]

Morton submitted a report to the lighthouse board on September 30 describing the completion of construction:

There has been performed the most important work which I have been charged with viz the erection of a 1st order Light House Tower, and Keeper's dwelling.

The tower is of brick, with a granite cornice, and rests upon a foundation of concrete faced with granite. There is…concrete under all of the above, which is 6 feet thick and 50 feet in diameter, and thus give an ample bearing and support to the superstructure.

The bed of this concrete is about a foot below low water, and the brick work of the tower commences at the level of 14 feet above mean tide.

From the foot of the tower proper to the top of the cornice is 140 feet, and the focal plane of the lens is 12 feet above the last mentioned level, so that the light is about 166 feet above the mean level of the sea.

A substantial stone dwelling of one-story and attic has also been built containing a large oil room, and separate quarters for 3 keepers and their families. This communicates with the tower, and with the exterior as well as with the main hall of the dwelling. There is a terrace around the entire premises, which is embanked to the level of 13 feet above mean tide. This terrace is retained by a wall of dry masonry, the material of which were obtained from the demolition of the old tower and keeper's house.

The tower is round and tapers very rapidly below.…The upper portion runs up nearly cylindrical. The curve used to determine the shape was a hyperbolar.

The cornice is of Doric order, and is joined to the tower by six pilasters which spring vertically from the inclined face of the tower.

The tower is ascended by spiral stairs; the tread of cast iron open work, rest on wrought iron pieces, and these are supported by the cylindrical wall of the Tower and by a cast iron central hollow column.

The tower is fitted with an illuminating apparatus of the 1ˢᵗ order revolving catadiptric [an optical system in which refraction and reflection are combined] *of the system of Fresnel, which produces a brilliant flash (of white light) once a minute. The weights belonging to the clock work descend inside of the central iron column.*

The lens was manufactured by the Henry Lepaute Company in France in 1857 and imported by the Ames Company of Chicopee, Massachusetts. The cost to the government was $15,000. The glass lens was eight feet, five inches tall with a diameter of six feet, seven inches. Each of the eight sides had three sections: a cone-shaped top consisting of prisms, a center section with a bull's-eye panel and prisms and the lowest section made of prisms. It sat on a base that was eight feet, two inches high. It weighed four tons. It was illuminated initially by a circular five-wick oil lamp and later upgraded to an incandescent oil vapor lamp. It is believed that the original fuel was whale oil, which was the standard fuel used by the lighthouse service at the time. Over the years, other fuel sources were colza or rapeseed oil, kerosene, lard oil and mineral oil. The lens captured 80 percent of the light emitted by the lamp into a beam visible out twenty miles. It emitted a five-second flash and then was dark for fifty-five seconds while revolving once every eight minutes. Winding the clockworks mechanism would lift the weights in the central iron column and keep the lens rotating for about four hours.

The keeper's dwelling built by Morton was a Tudor–Gothic Revival structure with deep eaves located south of the lighthouse and facing south toward the ocean. It had a slate gable roof with clipped ends, known as a jerkin-head roof. A chimney that had been situated at the peak of the southern portion of the building was removed at some point later. The walls were made of cut stone in a random ashlar, or square, pattern. The keeper's family lived on the west side, with a kitchen and sitting room on the first floor and two large bedrooms upstairs. Each of the two assistants had a kitchen downstairs on the east side of the building and two bedrooms upstairs, one large and one small. (Smith would get a second assistant, Samuel M. Smith, on March 19, 1859, easing the load on the keeper and first assistant Stephen Fordham.) Initially, there were no bathrooms. The three keepers and their families relied instead on a brick privy 5 feet by 8 feet just to the north of the tower. The dwelling was built on a raised terrace of stone and brick 100 by 147 feet. In his September 30 report, Morton said the terrace was at "a level of 13 feet above mean tide. The terrace is retained by a wall of dry stone masonry, the materials of which

NOTICE TO MARINERS.

FIRE ISLAND LIGHT-HOUSE.

LONG ISLAND, NEW YORK.

New Light-house Tower, 150 feet in height, fitted with a first order revolving Fresnel lens illuminating apparatus.

On the evening of Monday, the 1st day of November next, a *first order revolving light* will be exhibited for the first time, and on every night thereafter from sunset to sunrise, from the light-house tower now in course of erection at Fire Island Beach, east side of Fire Island inlet, south side of Long Island, N. Y. The illuminating apparatus is of the first order revolving catadioptric of the system of Fresnel, and will produce a brilliant *flash once in every minute*, which will not be materially different in appearance from the existing light in the old tower at that place, except in the greater brightness of the flash and increased range of the new light.

The light-house tower, which is placed about 200 feet N. E. from the old light-house tower, is built of brick, will be 150 feet in height, of a cream or yellow color, and the light will be about 166 feet above the mean level of the sea.

The old light-house tower and keepers' dwelling will be removed immediately after the exhibition of the light from the new tower.

The new light should be seen in ordinary states of the atmosphere, from the deck of a vessel 15 feet above the water, from 21 to 23 nautical miles.

Approximate position of the new light-house tower:

Latitude, 40° 37′ 53″ North.
Longitude, 73° 12′ 51″ West.

Distances from Fire Island light-house, to—

Montauk Point Light-house, 67½ nautical mil s.
Great West Bay Light-house, 35 " "
Sandy Hook Light vessel, - 31 " "
Navesink Lights, - - - 37½ " "
Barnegat Light-house, - - 66 " "

By order of the Light-house Board:

J. ST. C. MORTON,
U. S. Corps Engineers.

ENGINEER'S OFFICE,
Third L. H. District, New York, July 3, 1858.

A "Notice to Mariners" on July 3, 1858, about the impending inauguration of the second Fire Island Lighthouse. *Courtesy of the National Archives and Records Administration.*

were obtained from the demolition of the old tower and Keeper's house."[30]

Today, all that remains above ground of the original lighthouse is several feet of the circular bottom of the tower, which can be seen to the west of the new lens building.[31]

Well before the work was completed, the board began the process of notification about the pending change in the aid to navigation. It published a "Notice to Mariners" on July 3 signed by Morton that stated the new tower would be illuminated on November 1. It added that "the first order revolving catadioptric of the system of Fresnel…will produce a brilliant flash once in every minute, which will not be material different in appearance from the existing light in the old tower at that place, except in the greater brightness of the flash and increased range of the new light." The notice pointed out that the lighthouse would be sixty-seven and a half nautical miles from the Montauk Point Lighthouse, thirty-five miles from the beacon at Ponquoque to the east and thirty-one miles from the Sandy Hook Lightship at the entrance to New York Harbor.[32]

The first-order Fresnel light was lit for the first time by keeper Smith on November 1 as planned. Three days after the beacon—the tallest in New York State—was placed into service, Morton wrote to Franklin that "the light was duly exhibited on the first instant and burned excellently."[33]

The question of whether the new excellently bright light would make travel along the coast safer remained to be answered.

5

THE EARLY YEARS

Finding men willing to work at the taller lighthouse in the remote location wasn't always easy. A succession of keepers—some of them colorful characters—came and went.

Benjamin Smith, who had illuminated the second tower for the first time in 1858, left three years later. David Baldwin, who had started as second assistant keeper in 1862, moved up to the top job in January 1864. One of his first assistant keepers was Frank Wright, who had the distinction of being the father of Phoebe, the first baby born at the second lighthouse, on May 4, 1864, according to records at the light station. Her father was "removed" from his post on October 18, 1864, for reasons unknown. Phoebe grew up to marry Frank Clock, son of Nathanial Oakley Clock, who was the skipper of one of the America's Cup racing sailboats. Another first assistant keeper under Baldwin was Aaron Burr. (He was not the former vice president who shot Alexander Hamilton in a duel.) When the government decided to remove Baldwin in May 1865 for unknown reasons, finding a replacement proved difficult. The lighthouse board ran newspaper ads and put up notices in post offices but failed to attract any applicants. Apparently, a frustrated lighthouse board official traveled to Bay Shore and learned there was a lot of sentiment on the South Shore that the lighthouse might topple in a storm. Eventually, the local postmaster recommended that the official contact J.E. Hulse of Bay Shore, owner of a small fleet of boats. After much discussion, Hulse agreed to take the job—on one condition: he would not climb the spiral stairs inside the tower. When the official said he would be useless if he couldn't climb the tower every night to light the lamp, Hulse replied that he would rig a boom with a boatswain's, or bosun's, chair from the gallery below the lantern room. Then he would have his wife and daughters hoist him up each day at sunset and then let him down the same way in the morning. Hulse reportedly said, "If it falls over, I can die in the open, and not in that brick tunnel. That's my proposition, so take it or leave it." Hulse was appointed in May 1865, and the Patchogue native tended the light for almost four years.[34]

Early photo of the 1858 tower before it got its black and white stripes in the 1890s. *Courtesy of the National Archives and Records Administration.*

The light station seemed a little less remote when the Western Union Telegraph Company constructed a station nearby between 1868 and 1870. Its purpose was to notify shipping interests in New York City of arriving vessels. Those staffing it provided more human interaction for the keepers and their families. A telegraph apparatus was installed at the top of the lighthouse in January 1878 for the same purpose. The president of Western Union had written the lighthouse board the previous July for permission. He said that putting a telegraph key on the balcony of the lighthouse connected by wire to the telegraph station an eighth of a mile away would save at least fifteen minutes if the company observer did not have to run down the tower and back to the station to transmit. He promised that the company employees involved would be "experienced, careful, and trusty men whose conduct will conform to all the regulations of the service." The telegraph was later moved to the cupola of the Surf Hotel to the east. The telegraph building was destroyed by the Great Hurricane of September 21, 1938.[35]

Lighthouse board reports show the tower in good condition in 1869, but the illuminating apparatus required some attention. A new lamp was placed at the top of the tower that most likely burned a different fuel, probably colza oil.[36]

HARPER'S
NEW MONTHLY MAGAZINE.

No. CCLXXXVI.—MARCH, 1874.—Vol. XLVIII.

THE LIGHT-HOUSES OF THE UNITED STATES.
By CHARLES NORDHOFF.

THE first act of Congress relating to light-houses was passed August 7, 1789. It provided that "all expenses which shall accrue from and after the 15th day of August, 1789, in the necessary support, maintenance, and repairs of all light-houses, beacons, buoys, and public piers, erected, placed, or sunk before the passing of this act, at the entrance of or within any bay, inlet, harbor, or port of the United States, for rendering the navigation thereof easy and safe, shall be defrayed out of the Treasury of the United States."

Seven months later, March 26, 1790, the same words were re-enacted, but with a proviso that "none of the said expenses shall continue to be so defrayed by the United States after the expiration of one year from the day aforesaid, unless such light-houses, beacons, buoys, and public piers shall in the mean time be ceded to and vested in the United States by the State or States respectively in which the same lie, together with the lands and tenements thereunto belonging, and *together with the jurisdiction of the same.*"

Before this the States which possessed sea-ports had controlled and supported each its own light-houses; by these two acts Congress prepared to assume the control of these aids to navigation and commerce, as the Constitution required; and ever since the Federal government has not only maintained and supported the light-houses, but it has also owned them, and a sufficient space of ground about them for all necessary ends. And thus it was that in the first proclamation of Mr. Lincoln, in 1861, he announced his purpose to recover and maintain possession of all forts, *light-houses*, etc.

The Federal government has not in any case erected a light-house until the State government had first ceded both the land on which it was to stand and the jurisdiction over it.

FIRE ISLAND LIGHT, NEW YORK.

Entered according to Act of Congress, in the year 1874, by Harper and Brothers, in the Office of the Librarian of Congress, at Washington.

A March 1874 *Harper's New Monthly Magazine* article featuring an illustration of the Fire Island Lighthouse. *Courtesy of James W. Claflin.*

One of the more colorful keepers was appointed in January 1873. Hugh Walsh, who got the job after two years as an assistant, was described by boat builder Ralph Munroe as a "one-legged [keeper] appointed on political grounds rather than for fitness." Munroe wrote that one day, assistant keepers William J. Bailey and John Burke had gone across the bay and not returned by late afternoon. The keeper began to get frantic because

Walsh relied on one of his assistants for all mechanical details, and on this day of their absence he had foolishly taken the lamp apart for cleaning; about half an hour before lighting up he discovered that the big glass chimney and the sheet iron one were out of alignment. This was easy to correct with the three leveling screws under the font, but losing his head, he attempted to bend the sheet-iron pipe, nearly wrecking it; then remembering that I was something of a mechanic, he fairly jumped the whole of the iron stairway down the tower—180 feet—and I can see him now coming along the beach with the sand flying from his crutch, one leg and a cane. I met him partway, and hurrying back ahead of him, had the lamp connected and ready for him to light just in time to save his billet.[37]

Keeper Seth R. Hubbard had an on-again off-again relationship with the lighthouse. He started as an assistant in 1869–70 and returned again

Portrait of an early keeper, possibly Seth Hubbard, who served at the lighthouse from 1873 to 1881. *Courtesy of the Fire Island National Seashore.*

as second assistant and then first assistant in 1873–74 before becoming keeper that year and remaining until 1881. He was a Civil War veteran who had reportedly been a Union spy. His mother-in-law had cared for his wife and two children while he served, and when he returned, he wanted to do something to repay her. He purchased bricks and built an outdoor oven so she could bake bread. Hubbard's granddaughter, Grace Smith Hume of Far Rockaway in Queens, who was also the great-granddaughter of 1840s keeper Eliphalet Smith, visited the lighthouse in 1983 to tell family stories about the Fire Island beacon. Hume said her mother, Sara, had grown up at the lighthouse. And one night she operated it. "Once,

A January 9, 1875 article in the *Illustrated Christian Weekly* about a visit to the lighthouse. *Courtesy of James W. Claflin.*

when my mother was a little girl, she had to keep the lighthouse one night in a storm," Hume said. Her father had gone across the Great South Bay to Bay Shore for supplies and to pick up two lighthouse inspectors. But a storm prevented them from returning to the lighthouse. So twelve-year-old Sara and the assistant keeper were alone as darkness fell. "The assistant got into the liquor cabinet that they had to revive people caught in sea emergencies, and he was a little imbibed," Hume said. "So Sara decided that she would keep the light." That meant spending the night at the top of the tower equipped only with blankets, water and some crackers. She lay down on the blankets she had placed over the trapdoor to keep the drunk assistant keeper

at bay, adjusted the lamp wicks and raised the weights on the clockwork mechanism that rotated the lens as needed. "Her father could see that the light stayed lighted all night, and the government inspectors never found out about the assistant. But it was a night Sara never forgot," her daughter said.[38]

To make it easier for keepers at the top of the tower to communicate with those on the ground, speaking tubes like those on ships were installed in the 1870s. By 1876, the tower and its illuminating apparatus needed repairs. A new cement wash was applied to keep the lighthouse the desired yellow hue.[39]

Walter B. Abrams served as second assistant keeper and then first assistant keeper from 1884 to 1885. He married Josephine Hubbard in September 1885 when she was fourteen. He met her at the lighthouse, and they courted on the gallery outside the watch room while he was on duty. George W. Ruland became second assistant keeper in 1885 when his wife was pregnant. When she went into labor at the lighthouse, Abrams, the first assistant,

The Cunard liner *Oregon. Courtesy of the Dan Berg Wreck Valley Collection.*

rowed a lifeboat across the bay to Bay Shore, picked up Dr. William Hulse and rowed him back to deliver Floyd Ruland on May 25.[40]

The 1886 wreck of the transatlantic steamship *Oregon* led to placement of a lightship—a floating lighthouse—off the shore of Fire Island for the first time. *Oregon*, built in 1881 for the Guion Line, was 518 feet long, making it one of the largest vessels of its day. Constructed in the transition era between sail and steam, *Oregon* was powered by a three-cylinder engine but also fitted with four masts and sails. It set a speed record for an Atlantic crossing on its maiden voyage. In 1884, after Guion went bankrupt, the ship was sold to the Cunard Line. On March 6, 1886, *Oregon* departed Liverpool for New York. At 4:30 a.m. on March 14, in clear weather five miles off Fire Island, the ship was traveling at full speed when it collided with another vessel. It was believed to be the three-masted schooner *Charles R. Moss* of Maine, which was reported missing that night. Passenger John Hopkins of Brooklyn told the *New York Times* that "I heard a crash and felt a shock that shook the *Oregon* from end to end." He saw crewmen leaning over the port rail near the bow looking at a hole large enough to accommodate a horse and wagon. The schooner sank so quickly that no one aboard could be rescued. Captain Philip Cottier had distress rockets fired while the crew tried to stem the flooding in the largest watertight compartment located below the dining salon. Officer John Huston was credited with jumping into the ocean to save 2 children who fell in while being transferred to lifeboats. The pumps managed to keep the ship afloat for eight hours. That was sufficient time for all 845 passengers and crew to be rescued by the vessels *Fannie A. Gorhan*, *Fulda* and *Phantom*. There was even enough time for the crew to serve the passengers hot tea and toast before abandoning ship. Captain Cottier was the last to leave before *Oregon* sank bow-first.

The tops of *Oregon*'s masts and smokestacks remained above the surface, posing a hazard to navigation. So lightship LV *20*, which was then serving as a relief vessel for New York Harbor light vessels undergoing repairs, was dispatched to mark the site. LV *20* was constructed in 1867 in Greenpoint, Brooklyn. The wooden-hull ship was eighty-one feet long with two masts, and its only means of propulsion was sails. The vessel was rebuilt in 1880 and the lamps upgraded to burn kerosene. The lightship left Fire Island in late 1886 after the *Oregon*'s stacks and masts were dismantled.

After a hearing by the Liverpool Board of Inquiry, *Oregon*'s captain was held responsible for the collision and relieved from duty. LV *20* ended its career in Connecticut and Massachusetts before being sold in 1923

SINKING OF THE STEAMSHIP **OREGON** OF THE CUNARD LINE

By collision with an unknown Schooner off the Coast of Long Island, on her voyage from Liverpool to New York, on Sunday Morning, March 14th, 1886, and Rescue of the Passengers, Officers and Crew (845 persons) by the Steamship FULDA of the North German Lloyds Line, Pilot Boat Phantom and Schooner Fannie A. Gorham.

A Currier and Ives engraving of the sinking of the *Oregon* off Fire Island in 1886. *Library of Congress*.

Masts of the *Oregon.*

LIGHT-SHIP MOORED APRIL 10 TO MARK THE WRECK OF THE "OREGON."

A *Harper's Weekly* engraving of the lightship placed temporarily near the wreck of the *Oregon* to warn other ships of its presence. *Courtesy of James W. Claflin.*

and reportedly used to store whiskey during Prohibition. Eventually, the vessel was burned in a Fourth of July celebration. Today, the broken-up remains of the *Oregon* lie in about 130 feet of water about twenty-one miles southeast of Fire Island Inlet. It is considered the premier Long Island wreck site by divers.[41]

While the taller Fire Island Lighthouse was keeping mariners safer, it increased casualties of another kind. As was the case with other illuminated towers lining the nation's coastlines, the Fire Island Lighthouse was responsible for cutting short the lives of numerous birds. This was no secret to ornithologists, some of whom worked with lighthouse keepers to accumulate information that might reduce the mortality rate. William Dutcher, later a founder and first president of the National Audubon Society, developed connections with keepers in the New York City area. On September 23, 1887, when there was a massive bird strike at Fire Island, keeper E.J. Udall alerted Dutcher. He wrote that "a great bird wave...rolling southward along the Atlantic" came by the lighthouse, and he counted 595 dead birds at the foot of the tower the next morning. Udall didn't stop there: he shipped all of the birds to Dutcher for examination. The ornithologist identified twenty-five species, including the western form of a female palm warbler, the first ever of its kind recorded on Long Island.[42]

The same year that Udall was counting dead birds, the slate roof tiles on the dwelling were replaced by shingles because the slate was too difficult to maintain.[43]

After working at the Strafford Shoal Light in the middle of Long Island Sound and on lightships, Ezra S. Mott became keeper at Fire Island in the summer of 1888. Mott, forty-three, had started out as a farmer before getting involved in local shipping and becoming part owner of three vessels. He and his wife, Melissa, who had been married in Port Jefferson in 1869, had four daughters: Mary, Lucy, Evilyn and Melissa. After only five months on the job, Mott, who was known to be a conscientious employee and was well liked by those in the area, was under scrutiny by his superiors. They were questioning why the lighthouse was consuming so much oil. In November, according to Mott's records, the beacon had exceeded the monthly allowance by 19 percent. The district lighthouse inspector sent lamp expert Joseph Funck to Fire Island to investigate. He confirmed that Mott's measurements were

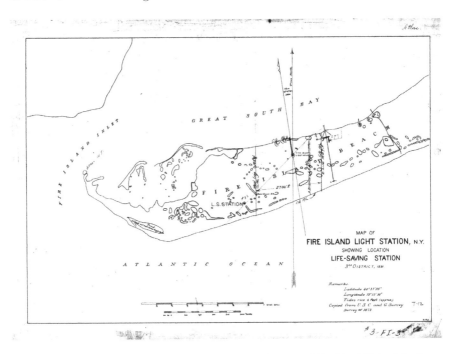

An 1891 map of Fire Island showing the light station. *Courtesy of Fire Island National Seashore.*

accurate and the lamp was, in fact, burning more oil than expected. He determined this was the result of an increase in the lantern room draft caused by the installation of pipes for that purpose and the replacement of the burner on the lamp with one that had larger oil supply tubes. While burning more fuel, the lamp produced a larger and brighter flame. The Fire Island flame was five inches high, while the lamp specifications stipulated a flame three and a half to three and three-quarters high. Since the lighthouse was "the most important one in this district if not on the whole Sea-Coast," Mott was told to "maintain the highest flame…without regard to the quantity of oil consumed."[44]

While the lamp arrangement was not changed, a major alteration to the exterior of the tower came three years later. On August 6, 1891, Commodore James A. Greer, chairman of the lighthouse board, published a "Notice to Mariners" that stated that the color of the tower would be "changed from yellow to alternate bands of black and white, two of each color." Each of the bands would be about thirty-five feet high. The change was designed to make the lighthouse more visible and easily identifiable in daytime. That color scheme remains to this day.[45]

Other changes came to the light station over the years in the form of additional outbuildings. A boathouse, fourteen by thirty feet, with a shingled roof and batten sides was constructed in 1888. A coal house and an oil house were also erected. The following decade, the lighthouse board proposed an electrifying change. The 1894 annual report explained that the Fire Island beacon remained "the most important light for transatlantic steamers bound for New York. It is generally the first one they make and from which they lay their course." It noted that the first-order light was illuminated by an oil lamp of 500 candlepower with the intensity of the flash equal to 63,830 candles. The report continued:

Mr. Henry Lepaute, of Paris, France, a manufacturer of lens apparatus for light-houses, exhibited at the World's Columbian Exposition, held in Chicago in 1893, what is known as a bivalve lightning light, with electricity as an illuminant. It is called bivalve because it consists of two powerful range lenses, 9 feet in diameter, back to back, and is named a lightning light on account of the brilliancy and short duration of the flash. The Arc light used is of very high candle power, and the makers claim that the intensity of the flash will be proportionately greater. The apparatus is so arranged as to give a flash every five seconds. The duration of the flash is about one-tenth of a second. The Light-House Board concluded to

*purchase this apparatus and install it in Fire Island light tower in place of
the present lens.*

Replacing the lighting apparatus required construction of an engine house
to contain a steam and electric-light plant with a boiler. That structure was
under construction when the report was written. A letter from the U.S. Army
Corps of Engineers to the treasury secretary on May 17, 1894, discussed
substituting the new electric light and noted that "the electric lighting of Fire
Island is in the nature of an experiment. This light, when established, will
be the only one of its kind in the United States, and it is of great importance
that, on account of imperfect machinery, risk of failure be avoided. To this
end, the best and not the cheapest appliances should be purchased, and the
engines, boilers, dynamos and electric fittings should be obtained from firms
who are positively known to be reliable."

By the end of the next fiscal year, on June 30, 1895, a powerhouse with
an arched roof and a skylight and a coal shed had been built; two boilers, an
engine and a dynamo were in place; a cistern with a 10,500-gallon capacity
was created; and a 750-foot narrow-gauge railroad track had been built from

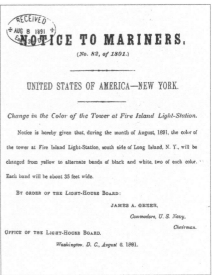

Left: Early photograph of the lighthouse with black and white bands. *Courtesy of Fire Island National Seashore.*

Right: A "Notice to Mariners" in 1891 about changing the color of the tower from yellow to black and white bands. *Courtesy of East Islip Public Library.*

the bay beach to the coal shed. But the bivalve light was never installed, and the electric power plant was never put into operation at Fire Island. The lighthouse board decided instead to station a lightship nine miles offshore. (See the next chapter.) The lightship did not arrive until July 20, 1896, and until then, the lighthouse was the sole aid to navigation. But a monthly report for October 1895 noted that the work had been suspended at the lighthouse, and the materials for the lens change had been transported to the regional maintenance depot in Staten Island. By December, the plant had been removed from Fire Island and brought to the depot.[46]

The land to the east of the light station was acquired by New York State in 1892. Officials purchased the old Surf Hotel and surrounding 125 acres for use as a quarantine station for European immigrants on an approaching ship who reportedly had cholera. The hotel was a large resort served twice daily by a paddle-wheel steamboat from Babylon. The Surf was built in the 1860s and survived for its first three decades by hosting many celebrities and politicians. Residents of Babylon and Islip opposed the quarantine station. Several boatloads of them crossed the bay, planning to burn the hotel to the ground. They were thwarted when the caretaker refused to evacuate his family, so instead they occupied the dock and prevented the landing of the first shipload of immigrants, who, it turned out, did not have the disease. After a unit of state militia arrived to disperse the demonstrators, the hotel was used for a year as a quarantine station. In 1908, it became Long Island's first state park: Fire Island State Park. The state would swap the land with the federal government for the Camp Hero military base in Montauk in 1985 so it could be added to Fire Island National Seashore.[47]

Communications between the keepers and the outside world got a boost with the first telephone connection on May 5, 1898, a month after the United States initiated the Spanish-American War. Although no enemy vessels ever came anywhere near Long Island, a line was run between the light station and the district lighthouse engineer's office under a special congressional appropriation for national defense. The light station closed out the century as the location for a series of experiments in wireless telegraphy by the War Department Signal Office after the lighthouse board approved the action in 1899.[48]

Despite all the technological improvements, the lighthouse board decided in the late 1800s that the Fire Island Light by itself was not sufficient to safely guide mariners along the barrier island. So it decided to place a lightship offshore to augment the tower.

6

THE FIRE ISLAND LIGHTSHIPS

By the mid-1890s, the transatlantic traffic to New York was booming. About 450,000 passengers and $676 million in cargo were arriving in the port annually. Concerned that all of these vessels could not navigate safely with the aid of the Fire Island Lighthouse alone, the U.S. Light-House Board placed a whistle buoy six miles offshore. But ship captains complained it was too small to see in poor weather and the whistle was not audible over the sounds of their engines.[49]

The lighthouse board responded by replacing the buoy with a lightship. This was an anchored floating lighthouse with the accommodations for the crew and equipment required to remain at its assigned location indefinitely. Food and other supplies were provided periodically by tender vessels. Three lightships in succession—all painted red with FIRE ISLAND emblazoned in white on their sides—would be deployed nine miles from shore to augment the tower from the 1800s until World War II.[50]

The first of these was LV *58*, which arrived in 1896 as the replacement for the scrapped plan to install the electrified bivalve lens at the lighthouse. The government had ordered construction of a new lightship, LV *68*, for Fire Island, and $80,000 had been appropriated for the project. But when construction was delayed, LV *58* was sent to Fire Island instead after having been stationed at Nantucket New South Shoal in Massachusetts since 1894.

The first Fire Island lightship was built by the Craig Shipbuilding Company of Toledo, Ohio, in 1893. The steel-hulled vessel was 121 feet, 10 inches long. Its one-cylinder steam engine could push it at seven and a half

The LV *58* was the first vessel to serve as a Fire Island lightship, from 1896 to 1897. It is painted here with the name *Relief*, as it later served as a relief lightship. *Courtesy of* Lighthouse Digest.

knots, and the vessel was also rigged with sails. Oil lamps in lanterns 39 feet above the waterline cast a fixed white light. A steam chime whistle backed by an emergency hand-rung bell was used in case of fog.

The light vessel remained off Fire Island Inlet for a year until LV *68* finally arrived. It then became a relief vessel in Massachusetts. While relieving LV *66* at Nantucket Shoals on December 10, 1905, LV *58* developed a leak during a heavy gale. After rising water extinguished the boilers and the suction pumps failed, the crew began to bail with buckets. The tender *Azalea* took the lightship in tow in heavy seas while the crew continued to bail. But the flooding worsened, and the order was given to abandon ship. The crew safely transferred to *Azalea*, and LV *58* sank less than ten minutes later.

LV *68* was built in Bath, Maine, with a wood bottom over a steel frame. It was 122 feet, 10 inches long. The one-cylinder steam engine propelled the ship at eight and a half knots, but it was also rigged with sails. For times of poor visibility, LV *68* was equipped with a steam chime and a one-thousand-pound bell rung by hand. Its two lanterns were mounted at a height of 57 feet, and the fixed white light came from clusters of three one-hundred-candlepower electric lamps that were changed to acetylene in 1920 and electricity in 1928. The lights were visible for thirteen miles.[51]

The vessel had some trouble remaining in its assigned location. LV *68* lost its anchor and chain in a storm on December 5, 1902. The ship steamed to Staten Island for replacements and was towed back the next day. On January 14, 1904, LV *68* again lost its anchor and chain and steamed to the depot for replacements and was towed back.[52]

The vessel encountered a much bigger problem in 1916 when it was rammed on May 8 by SS *Philadelphian*. The side of the lightship's hull was pushed in about two feet starting four feet below the waterline. Mate Julius Ortman and engineer Peter Hanson were slightly injured. The crew quickly began damage control, emptying water tanks, shifting coal and swinging out lifeboats on the undamaged side and filling them with water. These actions heeled the ship enough to keep much of the damaged area out of the water so the bilge pumps could keep it afloat. The *Philadelphian* towed LV *68* to the entrance of New York Harbor, where the tender *Pansy* took over and brought the light vessel to the Staten Island depot. A lightship tender temporarily replaced LV *68* that night, and a relief lightship took up the station the next day until the damaged vessel was repaired. The crew of *68* was commended by the secretary of commerce for saving the vessel.

In 1918, the crew participated in an unusual rescue when the log shows they "towed airplane with two occupants to ship." Three years later on May 1, 1921, LV *68* became one of the first three light vessels to be equipped with a radio beacon that ships could home in on in times of poor visibility. While these radio signals were a boon to fog-bound navigators at sea, they increased the danger for the lightships because the other vessels would sometimes follow the beacon right into the stationary aid to navigation.[53]

This apparently is what happened when LV *68* was rammed again on March 30, 1924. At 2:45 p.m., in dense fog, the English steamer *Castilian* struck the lightship, slicing a large hole from the upper deck to the waterline. The *Lighthouse Service Bulletin* noted that before the collision "all fog signals, steam whistle, submarine bell, and radio fog signal were in operation." The

The LV *68* was the second vessel to serve as the Fire Island lightship, from 1897 to 1930. *Courtesy of* Lighthouse Digest.

assistant engineer said he heard three ships nearby and went on deck to look for them. "I then heard a sudden rush of water coming straight towards us. I looked up and saw the steamer heading for us amidships. I then rang the alarm bell. Somehow or other the steamer sheared off and when I stopped ringing the alarm bell she struck the light vessel on the port quarter." The pumps were started. But they could not keep up with the water rushing in until the crew placed a patch made with planks and tarpaulins over the hole. Once again, LV *68* headed for Staten Island. On the way, it was met by the tender *Spruce*, which towed the crippled ship the rest of the way to the depot the next morning. LV *109*, which was about to be deployed off New Jersey, was at the depot. It was dispatched to Fire Island and took up station temporarily on March 31 until its sister ship could be repaired. Captain Frank Seastedt and the rest of the LV *68* crew received commendations for "rendering efficient service and showing fine seamanship and devotion to duty in standing by the ship after the collision." LV *68* remained off Fire Island until 1930, when it became a relief ship for two years before being auctioned off for $825.[54]

The final lightship off Fire Island was LV *114*. Built in 1930 in Portland, Oregon, it became the first light vessel in the history of the U.S. Lighthouse Service to be built on the West Coast and serve on the East Coast. The vessel was 133 feet long and made of steel. The 350-horsepower diesel-electric motor could push it at a cruising speed of nine knots. Like its two predecessors, *114* displayed a fixed white light from each mast, but the fog signal was powered by compressed air and backed by a hand-operated bell. The two electric lanterns were mounted at a height of 57 feet.[55]

The vessel was manned by five officers and ten crewmen. Captain J. Nielsen began the 5,892-mile journey to New York on July 15, 1930, and LV *114* was the first lightship to travel through the Panama Canal. The trip to the Staten Island depot took thirty-two days.

After the United States entered World War II following the December 7, 1941 Japanese attack on Pearl Harbor, Germany sent submarines to hunt off the American coast. The stationary lightships made attractive targets. The crew aboard LV *114* mentioned in the ship's log on Christmas Day 1941 that a lookout had spotted flares believed to have been fired by a prowling German U-boat. The government removed LV *114* from its station on January 11, 1942. Although fitted out for military service with armament and radar, it spent the duration of the war docked in Bay Shore. After peace returned, the lightship didn't resume its prewar duty. By then, large vessels had been equipped with radar, and lightships and even lighthouses had

The LV *114* sliding down the ways at Portland, Oregon, in 1930. It was the third and final Fire Island lightship. *Courtesy of* Lighthouse Digest.

Old postcard view of the MV *Britannic* passing Fire Island lightship LV *58*. *Courtesy of* Lighthouse Digest.

been reduced in importance. A buoy was stationed where the lightship once anchored. LV *114* was decommissioned in 1971 and acquired by the City of New Bedford, Massachusetts. In 2006, the ship developed a leak and rolled over on its side. The following year, it was sold for scrap.[56]

With the decision to no longer station a lightship off Fire Island, it was left to the lighthouse and buoys to point the way to New York Harbor. But three decades after the departure of LV *114*, the Fire Island Lighthouse itself would be deemed superfluous and extinguished.

Above: The tower readied for restoration in 1987. *Courtesy of Fire Island National Seashore.*

Left: Restoration of the tower in 1987. *Courtesy of* Lighthouse Digest.

Left: View of the ocean from the tower gallery. *Copyright 2016 Audrey C. Tiernan.*

Below: The lighthouse, keeper's dwelling and lens building. *Copyright 2016 Audrey C. Tiernan.*

Left: A view of the lighthouse from the Fire Island National Seashore boardwalk. *Copyright 2016 Audrey C. Tiernan.*

Below: The lighthouse rises over a dune. *Copyright 2017 Audrey C. Tiernan.*

The light station in winter. *Copyright 2017 Audrey C. Tiernan.*

Remnants of the foundation from the 1826 lighthouse. *Copyright 2016 Audrey C. Tiernan.*

The keeper's dwelling. *Copyright 2017 Audrey C. Tiernan.*

Circular window in keeper's dwelling framing the view of the beach and ocean. *Copyright 2016 Audrey C. Tiernan.*

The boathouse.
*Copyright 2016
Audrey C. Tiernan.*

Surf rescue car
used at Fire Island
on display in the
boathouse. *Copyright
2016 Audrey C.
Tiernan.*

A souvenir cup and
saucer showing
the Fire Island
Lighthouse, with
its pattern of black
and white bands
reversed, made in
Vienna, Austria, for
a Babylon, Long
Island company
about 1900 and
recently acquired
by the Fire Island
Lighthouse
Preservation Society.
*Copyright 2017 Audrey
C. Tiernan.*

Above: The view from the tower looking west showing the Atlantic Ocean on the left, the Great South Bay on the right, the water tower at Robert Moses State Park and the Robert Moses Causeway bridge. *Copyright 2016 Audrey C. Tiernan.*

Left: Team from The Lighthouse Consultant LLC reassembling the original first-order Fresnel lens in the new lens display building in 2011. *Photo by Joe Lachat.*

A fisheye-lens view from the top of the tower looking northwest with the lens building to the left, the boathouse to the right and the shadow of the tower in the middle. *Copyright 2016 Audrey C. Tiernan.*

Above: A view looking up the 156 spiral steps leading up from the base of the tower. The top 34 steps leading to the lantern room are in straight staircases. *Copyright 2016 Audrey C. Tiernan.*

Left: The three porthole windows near the top of the north side of the tower. *Copyright 2016 Audrey C. Tiernan.*

Left and above:
Various views
of the Fresnel
lens. *Copyright
2016 Audrey C.
Tiernan.*

The modern
airport beacon-
style light in the
tower. *Copyright
2016 Audrey C.
Tiernan.*

The original Fresnel lens in the lens building that opened in 2011. *Copyright 2016 Audrey C. Tiernan.*

The Fresnel lens and the keeper's quarters. *Copyright 2016 Audrey C. Tiernan.*

The lighthouse at dusk. *Copyright 2016 Audrey C. Tiernan.*

The lighthouse at sunset. *Copyright 2016 Audrey C. Tiernan.*

The lighthouse in the evening. *Copyright 2016 Audrey C. Tiernan.*

The top of the tower with stars. *Copyright 2016 Audrey C. Tiernan.*

1

FROM LIGHT TO DARK

A s the twentieth century opened, the Fire Island Lighthouse continued to receive technological upgrades. But that didn't stop maritime interests from lobbying for a more effective aid to navigation.

In response, the lamp was changed in 1907. A brighter incandescent oil vapor system replaced the oil lamp in early December. The new lamp flashed for four seconds and was dark for fifty-six seconds. The old lamp had emitted a five-second flash and then was dark for fifty-five seconds.

The improved lamp, however, was insufficient to mollify ship owners and marine insurance company executives who felt the illumination remained inadequate. They began circulating a petition the following year seeking to further boost the intensity of the light. Their petition pointed out that "the light on Fire Island is the objective point which is made by all vessels approaching New York Harbor from the East after making Nantucket South Shoal Light-Vessel....It is of the greatest importance to the safety, and the uninterrupted course, of navigation that the light on Fire Island should be of a character equal to that of the best lights in existence elsewhere....The present light on Fire Island...is not of such power as should be provided for a light in this important position." The lighthouse board was responsive and in its 1908 annual report repeated the language of the petition as its own position. It added that "it is estimated that the station can be equipped with modern high power illuminating apparatus at a cost of $30,000 and the Board recommends that an appropriation of that amount be made." But nothing was done to implement the recommendation.[57]

While the efficacy of the light was being discussed, the tower was deteriorating. Inspected in April 1912, it was found to have a large crack 130 feet above the ground, with smaller ones below. The lighthouse board's response was to install metal mesh and reinforcing bands around the tower and apply a new protective coating.[58]

There was an addition to the grounds around 1906 when the navy received permission to establish a radio–direction finding station for determining the position of vessels at sea. It would be turned over to the Coast Guard in 1941.[59]

Dealing with the isolation continued to be a problem for some of those stationed at the light station, especially keepers without a family. First assistant keeper Hans Christian Anderssen, who came to Fire Island in August 1910, tried a unique approach to deal with his loneliness: he asked newspaper reporters to write about his search for a bride. They complied. The keeper, the *Brooklyn Daily Eagle* wrote, "having followed the sea all his life, has not much opportunity to secure a helpmeet. He heard somewhere that advertising is one of the things that bring success—so he tried it." The paper described him as "a stoutly built man of 38. His face is jolly and his mustache is of a sandy color. He is an earnest talker, who sees nothing very ludicrous in advertising for a better half." The paper noted he was born in Sweden and received his early education in France. Anderssen was not encouraged by the initial response. In a mixture of Swedish, French and English he told a reporter in June 1911 that "it didn't do no good. I got over 50 answers but all of them were so awful old. One was 60—I don't want anybody like that." He did say that three young women about age twenty-two responded, but he didn't like them. He added that "it is lonely over here—there ain't many people. Then I get tired of cooking—I don't like to cook. That's the reason I eat the cold ham and the canned beans....I ain't trying to get no wife now. I think I will let it drop. Advertising don't pay, I guess, in the marrying business."

But the responses kept coming because of all the newspaper coverage. And on October 22, the *Eagle* wrote that "now that he is happily wedded, he advises all who need a 'helpmeet' to advertise also." Ultimately, Anderssen received replies from more than two hundred women from ages fifteen to sixty:

> *All offered to learn to love him. Every last one of them was a fine cook, a good-looking damsel, or matron, of an affectionate temperament, who just doted on lighthouses and the sea. They all knew (through some*

—Oct. 5

Restoration of the tower in 1912. *Courtesy of the U.S. Lighthouse Society Archive.*

feminine form of second sight) that Anderssen was a man that they could love—really and truly love with the whole ardor of their first heart consuming passion—or something like that. By a process of elimination, Anderssen selected the best of the whole collection and on Monday was married to Mrs. Blanche Mitchuel, a 19-year-old French woman, who is a widow. Therefore Anderssen is happy.

But not for long.

An article the following January carried a headline of "Wife Won by 'Ad' Sues." Blanche had gone to the state supreme court seeking a legal separation and appointment of a guardian for her child by her previous marriage. In the court papers, Mrs. Anderssen said her husband was addicted to drink and frequently beat her. By the time the article was written, Anderssen had been transferred upstate to a lighthouse on Lake Champlain.[60]

Whether or not Anderssen was really an abusive drunk, some keepers had a troubled tenure, either because of the isolation or inherent personality problems. Most notably, Norman B. Devine "went insane" in 1926, according to a lighthouse board report. His tenure ended that year.

While not succumbing to madness, William F. Aichele had a rocky time after his appointment as keeper on October 1, 1909. Aichele apparently was a bad manager who did not know how to get along with people. He was reprimanded in a letter from the Third District inspector on March

A U.S. Lighthouse Service badge displayed in the keeper's quarters museum. The Lighthouse Service was created in 1910. *Copyright 2016 Audrey C. Tiernan.*

26, 1912. It stated that the "difficulty between yourself and the assistant Keepers is due to your lack of enforcement of discipline at the station." A follow-up letter two weeks later added that "it has been noted from inspection report of Fire Island Light-Station that the two assistant keepers are unable to perform their share of work of painting tower on account of nervousness. As this work is part of keepers and assistant keepers duties, assistant keepers should do their proportionate share of same. And you are hereby directed to have the assistant keepers do so, or else employ at their expense substitutes to perform this duty for them." The letter does not explain why the assistant keepers were nervous, although working on the higher reaches of the tower with the often strong ocean

Keeper George J. Thomas, who served from 1913 to 1919, his wife and two daughters, Lucy and Alice. *Courtesy of Fire Island National Seashore.*

breezes might explain it. In any case, Aichele didn't resolve his personnel problems. In 1914, his first assistant, Chester B. Harper, requested a transfer because of friction with his superior. The district inspector wrote to Aichele in May that "this office is of the opinion that the differences existing between yourself and the Asst. Keeper of the Station are due to petty and personal quarrels. You are informed that the continuance of such a condition will not be tolerated." The keeper was instructed to ensure that there would be "harmony and efficiency at the station." That did not happen, and Harper was dismissed rather than transferred in September.[61]

Aichele appears to have gotten along better with another one of his assistants, George J. Thomas, who started as second assistant in 1913. The men were cribbage partners and would play against men who staffed the nearby Western Union and Postal Telegraph towers. The winning team received a roast beef dinner.[62]

Reports filled out by Aichele now in the archives of Fire Island National Seashore document the wide range of supplies necessary to run the lighthouse. A "Keepers Annual Property Return, Annual Requisition, and Receipt" booklet Aichele submitted in 1916 spells out in minute detail the items on hand and needed for the following year. The keeper stated he had seventeen official-size envelopes on hand and needed fifty more. He had one lead pencil and needed two more. He wanted ten vials each of engine oil and clock oil. He requested forty cakes of soap and required seventy gallons of white paint, nine of black paint and five of cream color. The form spells out needed parts for the lamp vaporizer nozzle, mantles and kerosene and alcohol to keep the light illuminated.

While at Fire Island, Aichele's wife gave birth to two sons: Fritz and Hans, born about 1912 and 1915, respectively. Fritz would later become a charter boat captain out of Shinnecock Bay, and Hans became a Southampton police officer. Being surrounded by a growing family did nothing to resolve Aichele's personnel management problems. In 1916, district officials offered him a transfer to the less critical and stressful Crown Point Light on Lake Champlain. He accepted and left the following year.[63]

Thomas was promoted to keeper in July 1917 and served in that position until April 1919. Among his experiences was rescuing two aviators from a "sinking hydroplane" on the Great South Bay in 1918 and taking them to Bay Shore. That year he also helped extinguish a fire that destroyed several cottages and fishing shacks on the barrier island.[64]

Thomas's daughter Lucy returned to the lighthouse in May 1987 to donate artifacts, including photographs, a cribbage board her father used

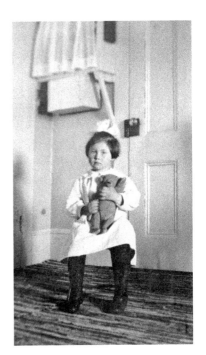

Right: Two-year-old Lucy Thomas in the second assistant keeper's quarters. *Courtesy of Fire Island National Seashore.*

Below: Cradle used by Lucy and Alice Thomas, daughters of George J. Thomas, keeper at Fire Island from July 1917 until April 1919, on display in the keeper's dwelling museum. *Copyright 2016 Audrey C. Tiernan.*

to pass the time and two porcelain dolls, one from Germany and the other from Japan. "The Japanese dolls came into favor when we were first at war with Germany in 1914," Thomas explained as she reminisced with a Fire Island National Seashore ranger. The most important donation was the cradle used by Lucy and her younger sister Alice, who was born in Brooklyn on November 19, 1915, and brought home to the lighthouse when she was two weeks old.

Thomas recounted that her father made her wear a wide-brimmed red straw hat when she was wandering around the island so it would be easy to keep an eye on the inquisitive and fearless girl from the top of the lighthouse. One day, she recalled, she climbed aboard the scow that had just ferried ashore a year's worth of coal, paint and other provisions from a ship anchored offshore. Lucy, then five, had managed to push the scow back into the water and shoved off using a stick as a paddle. When her family could not immediately find her, someone went up the tower and saw her headed toward the channel leading to Bay Shore. Planning to go there to buy her father a box of candy, she was brought back without mishap.

Lucy Thomas left Fire Island in the fall of 1917 to attend school in Brooklyn, where she lived with relatives. But later that year, there was an influenza epidemic in which people were "killed off like flies, so I was yanked out of second grade and sent to the beach." Her mother made sure she kept up with her studies at the light station.

Thomas talked about how she enjoyed walking with her father along the ocean beach, which was much wider and had bigger dunes when she was growing up in the keeper's quarters. One afternoon in 1918, she heard the sound of an explosion out to sea. "It happened too far offshore to see," she remembered. Later she learned it came from the USS *San Diego*, a navy cruiser that had run into a mine laid by a German U-boat in World War I.

The 503-foot, 11-inch *San Diego* was launched as USS *California* in 1904 in San Francisco. But it had not been commissioned into the U.S. Navy until 1907. After sailing as part of Theodore Roosevelt's Great White Fleet, on September 1, 1914, the warship was renamed *San Diego* and served as the flagship for the Pacific fleet. On July 18, 1917, it was ordered to the Atlantic to escort convoys through the first dangerous leg of their journey to Europe. On July 8, 1918, the *San Diego* left Portsmouth, New Hampshire, for New York. At 11:23 a.m. on July 19, a mine believed to have been laid by *U-156* ripped a huge hole in the port side amidships. Captain Harley Christy immediately ordered the crew to their battle stations and the closing of all

USS *San Diego*, which sank after hitting a German mine off Fire Island in 1918 during World War I. *Author's collection.*

watertight doors. Soon there were two more explosions, later determined to be caused by the rupturing of a boiler and ignition of the armaments magazine. With the ship listing to port, guns were fired at what the crew thought might be a submarine periscope. With the ship settling and some guns already awash, Christy shouted an order: "All hands abandon ship!" He then had the ship steered toward Fire Island, hoping to beach it. But at 11:51 a.m., *San Diego* sank, twenty-eight minutes after the initial blast. In accordance with tradition, Christy was the last man off the vessel. As the vessel was rolling over, he made his way down from the bridge and jumped eight feet into the water. Crew in the lifeboats cheered him and started to sing "The Star-Spangled Banner" and "My Country 'Tis of Thee." Most of the sailors were picked up by other vessels, but at least four lifeboats were rowed ashore, three at Bellport and one near the Lone Hill Coast Guard Station. Six crewmen died aboard or in abandoning ship. The *San Diego* was the only major warship lost by the United States in the war. Today, the *San Diego* lies upside down in 110 feet of water, thirteen and a half miles southeast of Fire Island Inlet, where it is one of the two premier shipwrecks off the South Shore visited by divers.[65]

There were other reminders for Lucy Thomas that the ocean could be dangerous, particularly in wartime. Thomas said assistant keeper Edward

Painting by Frank Litter of the sinking of USS *San Diego*. *Courtesy of Frank Litter.*

A. Donahue, whose daughters Bebs and Mignon were her playmates, once pulled a live torpedo up on the beach. One of the items Thomas donated to the National Park Service was a silver tablespoon from the *Hougomont*, a freighter loaded with chalk that ran up on the sandbar near the lighthouse on February 16, 1915. "They got everyone off but the cook," she said. "He would not leave unless they would take his pig. Crewmen shoveled off some cargo to lighten the ship, which was raised by the next tide." One of the sailors gave George Thomas the spoon as a souvenir of the event. She also remembered another ship that ran ashore, the *Northern Pacific*, bringing wounded soldiers back from the war in 1919.

There were also bodies, or at least parts of bodies, that occasionally washed ashore. The Coast Guardsmen buried the remains between the lighthouse and their station. Sometimes, the wind would uncover them, and Lucy remembered the men would say that "the sailors are trying to go back to their ship."[66]

Even without a war going on, life at the lighthouse could be dangerous, as an incident in 1918 demonstrated. A little over five weeks after the sinking of the *San Diego*, the lighthouse was struck by lightning. On August 29, a bolt targeted the ball on the roof of the lantern. "It punctured a hole through the seam about 1 inch long and one-half inch wide," the lighthouse service reported. "It then went into the watch room and burned a small place on the column and followed down the call-bell wire to the hall of the dwelling and burned out the telephone wire and demolished the switch box connected with the telephone."[67]

For Lucy Thomas and the other women and girls living at the light station and nearby facilities, the main diversion was visiting each other. The arrival of a new baby was always a major event. Thomas said that one year, to relieve the boredom, the families held a costume party on Halloween. When it came to eating, the Thomases kept chickens for fresh eggs and had a vegetable garden that helped augment the supplies that came by boat. George Thomas had his own boat, a custom-built cabin cruiser named *Caroline* that the family used for trips to Bay Shore for shopping or to catch the train to New York.

When the freighter *Hougomont* ran up on the sandbar near the Fire Island Lighthouse on February 16, 1915, one of the sailors gave keeper George Thomas this silver spoon with the ship's name engraved on it. It is now in the Fire Island National Seashore archives. *Photo by the author.*

When there was a keeper and two assistants assigned at Fire Island, each would stand watch from an hour before sunset to midnight one night and then from midnight to dawn the second night, while the third would be off. After World War I began, there was only one keeper and one assistant, so they had little spare time. Thomas said that because her father had to stay awake all night, he would eat his big meal and sleep during the day. On winter nights, she would take a paper-bag supper up to her father with a lantern. A hemp line served as the railing around the spiral staircase. Warm Dutch apple cake was her father's favorite dessert. "There he would be, sitting on a Morris chair, reading the Bible, with a pile of other books and magazines beside him," she remembered. The keeper would spend the night in the watch room to make sure the light was shining properly and once an hour would wind the cable on the clockwork mechanism, which made the lens revolve. Illumination for reading came from a kerosene lamp on a wooden table. There was a wooden trapdoor in the middle of the floor to stop drafts. A metal ladder led up to the lantern room.

Every day, the keeper on duty would carry kerosene in a large brass can with a spout up the ladder to fill the lamp. The mantle of the light had to be primed with an alcohol flame that vaporized kerosene to feed the lamp for the night. The soot that accumulated on the glass lamp chimney and windows of the lantern room had to be cleaned regularly. "There was much polishing of glass and brass to keep things shipshape and sparkling," she said. Curtains had to be drawn in the lantern room during the day to shield the lens from the sun so a concentrated light beam would not ignite the lamp and create a fire.

As with earlier keepers and their families, the Thomases had to deal with birds, mostly ducks and geese, that crashed into the tower. Instead of sending them to an ornithologist, Lucy remembered taking wounded and dead birds to the Coast Guard station—where they were cooked and eaten—to supplement the fish, clams, oysters and scallops that were so readily available that they became boring.

Thomas recalled trips to the outhouse. The keeper's family had its own, and the assistant keepers shared one on the east side of the tower with two holes. (It was not until 1931 that the dwelling got indoor plumbing.)[68]

George Thomas left Fire Island in April 1919. After considering and then rejecting a posting upstate because of the meager living accommodations, in June he became second assistant keeper at the Shinnecock light station down the coast to the east. He was named keeper there that same year and remained until the light was extinguished on August 1, 1931. His daughter Alice later wrote an unpublished memoir of their life there. The document, in the archives at the Fire Island Lighthouse, provides a good idea of what life would have been like at the sister station to the west.

Besides their salaries, the three keepers also received a fuel allowance of seventeen tons of coal and one and a half cords of wood per year. Alice Thomas said the 168-foot-high lighthouse was repeatedly struck by lightning, but the copper lightning rod usually transmitted the charge harmlessly to the ground. "But one evening it went down the inside of the tower and out the front door. The accompanying noise was terribly frightening. All the paint inside the tower was scorched, but no one was hurt."

Work for the keepers was never-ending. Each morning at 8:00 a.m., the three keepers assembled in the hallway and proceeded up the tower, usually carrying a scuttle of coal, a five-gallon can of kerosene for the lamp and other supplies. The wick had to be trimmed and reservoir filled daily. All glass and brass in the lantern room was polished every day. Weather permitting, the exterior glass of the lantern was also cleaned. The clockwork mechanism that rotated the lens had to be inspected daily and oiled and the weights wound up every four hours while the light was in operation.

Alice described the watch room just below the lantern room:

> *There were no windows in this room, but there was a door which opened onto the catwalk which ran around the outside. The view from the catwalk was terrific. One could see far to sea, a lot of the bay....A ladder on one wall went to the lantern room, some cabinets around the wall held supplies, and a small "pot-belly" stove took up some space. A wooden "Morris" chair (the original adjustable back chair) and a table were the only furnishings. The table held a kerosene lamp, a "Big Ben" alarm clock, books, magazines, and an ash tray. Pop smoked a pipe....Paperbacks by Zane Grey were Pop's favorite reading material....I think he read all of the Bible while at Fire Island. It must have been hard at times to stay awake. There was no one to share the hours with and radio and TV had yet to be invented....However, the keeper on watch had to check the light frequently during the night plus wind up the weights. A daily report book was kept as to the weather and any unusual circumstance.*

Alice Thomas said there was a speaking tube from the lower hallway to the watch room so someone could communicate with the keeper on duty at the top of the tower without climbing all the stairs. But she said it did not work well and was rarely used. "Mainly Mom used it to tell Pop that Lucy or I was on the way up bringing some special dessert for supper and he would meet us part of the way," Alice wrote. "During a gale one at top of the tower could feel it sway. It was rather a peculiar feeling!"

During the day the keepers also had to maintain the buildings and grounds. One keeper raised the American flag on a tall flagpole and took it down at sunset. And there was always maintenance to do:

> *There was never ending brass polishing and window cleaning. In back of the tower there was a small brick "oil house" used to store kerosene, oil etc. All the measures [measuring cups] from an ounce to a gallon were brass, as well as all doorknobs in the hallway and outside doors of the dwellings. Lamps inside the houses also were brass and had to be cleaned, polished and filled. Floors were shellacked. Storm windows were put on dwelling windows in the fall and taken down in the spring. One thing or another always seemed to need painting.*

The inefficient fireplaces were kept closed off in the keeper's quarters, so the only heat came from a small potbelly stove in the dining room and the kitchen stove. "Not surprisingly, the building was cold in the winter," Alice wrote. She gives a vivid description of the chores undertaken by the women at Shinnecock and presumably Fire Island as well:

> One chore, not very pleasant but necessary, was to empty the barrels beneath the outhouses in the spring and fall.
>
> While the men had many chores to do, the women had an equal amount inside and outside the house. Mom would get up at 5 AM whether winter or summer. The first chore was to get the stoves fired up which had been "stoked" for the night, then letting the cat in and feed him. If it was bread making day, it was time to get it started. Soon Pop was up, dressed, and shaving at the kitchen sink. Lucy and I ran down in our night clothes in the winter to keep warm while we all had breakfast. Pancakes were a big favorite in wintertime....Beds had to be straightened...because you never knew when the lighthouse inspector might come.

There was also a daily list of chores:

> Monday was wash day and was one of the hardest days of the week. It was done in the cellar where there was another iron range, sink and water pump. First a good fire had to be established in the stove, the copper boiler placed on it and filled with pails of water. When the water was hot, it was bailed out to the big wooden washtub, and more water added to heat. The next tub had to be filled with water to rinse the clothes, and the final tub filled to which bluing was added to whiten the clothes. A wooden hand ringer was clamped on the final tub....Baskets of wet laundry had to be carried up steps and through the door to outside where there were long clothes lines made of cotton rope....In spring and summer birds with their droppings were a hazard; in winter the clothes froze practically as soon as they were hung up.
>
> Tuesday was ironing day. We had three...irons which were heated on the coal stove.
>
> Wednesday was mending and clothes making day....Mom made all her clothes as well as ours.... Sewing was done on a Singer treadle machine.... Not much was ever thrown away. Scraps of material were cut into one inch strips which were sewn together and rolled up. These were taken once a year to a weaver who made the rag rugs used in kitchen and bedrooms....

Thursday was a day for socializing.…

Friday was a day to make bread, cookies, cakes etc.…

Saturday was cleaning day.…Beds had to be changed, rugs taken out, floors dry or wet mopped, furniture dusted etc.…Later in the day was bath time. Hair was washed at the kitchen sink and dried outside when it was warm. The copper boiler was put on the stove and filled with water to heat, while the bathtub was brought up from the cellar and placed next to the stove. When everything was ready, Pop got to bathe first, followed by Lucy, then I, and finally Mom. More hot water was added between each.… Following the bath, we got clean clothes which hopefully would last until the following week.

Sunday was church day.

The two Thomas daughters make lighthouse life sound hard but wholesome and even somewhat romantic. But it wasn't that way for everyone. Aichele was not the only keeper with problems. Frank Oberley, who was appointed in 1919, was accused in 1921 of breaking into houses on the beach. He was arrested and held on $500 bail. The charges were dismissed when a grand jury failed to indict him. He left the lighthouse the following month.[69]

The U.S. Navy built a radio annex building about one thousand feet east of the lighthouse in 1921. The two-story masonry structure survives and is used by the National Park Service as a residence and office space.[70]

With Fire Island ever-growing westward, in 1924 the federal government turned over to the state the six hundred acres of land west of the lighthouse that had been deposited by littoral drift since construction of the first lighthouse. It was added to Fire Island State Park. Few people used it until 1926, when State Parks Commissioner Robert Moses reconstructed the whole area into Camp Cheerful, a facility for handicapped boys sponsored by the New York City Rotary Club. After the 1938 hurricane washed away all the facilities, Moses rebuilt the park—later named in his honor—more than two miles to the west.[71]

Keeper Isaac Karlin and his family were the first to enjoy the comfort of central heating, which was installed in the dwelling in 1927. Other changes followed. The oil house was destroyed in a 1929 fire. The boathouse was demolished in 1938 and rebuilt in the same location a year later. Then it was moved to the powerhouse foundation sometime after the powerhouse was demolished in 1956. The boathouse was returned to its original location by the bay in 2010. Between 1937 and 1939, various radio towers were constructed around the lighthouse. One three-hundred-foot-tall tower had

Keeper Isaac Karlin, who served from 1925 in 1928, with his family. *Courtesy of Fire Island National Seashore.*

the capability of reaching from Labrador to the Gulf of Mexico. A radio-beacon tower was erected on the beach around 1939 to broadcast a signal to help mariners navigate. And during World War II, the *Voice of America* broadcast from the light station. In 1937, the International Nickel Company of Delaware was given permission to occupy a section of the property for five years to test atmospheric weathering on sheet metals. Its facility occupied about 3.7 acres southwest of the lighthouse.[72]

From the 1890s through the early years of the twentieth century, the Fresnel lens and illumination equipment were continuously being repaired, even after the installation of the new vapor lamp in 1907. In 1929, the Office of the Superintendent of Lighthouses issued a recommendation stating that "the present apparatus is of obsolete type and is beyond economical repair; it has been giving trouble for several years and is now reached the point when replacement is necessary." The best way to do this was to transfer the lens and the mercury-filled basin that supported it from the discontinued Shinnecock Bay Light Station to Fire Island. That first-order lens, which was of a simpler design with four bull's-eye panels compared to the eight on the Fire Island Fresnel lens, was relocated. The Shinnecock lens, because it had fewer glass prisms, was lighter and could rotate faster and flash more frequently, improving its visibility for mariners. So while the old lens gave a five-second flash once a minute, the change allowed the lighthouse to flash every seven and a half seconds. After being lowered from the tower, the Fire Island lens was loaned to the Franklin Institute in Philadelphia for display in June 1933. The museum noted in its catalogue that the incandescent oil-vapor lamp produced a light of 280,000 candlepower, was located 167 feet above high water and could be seen for 19 miles.

In June 1938, the light apparatus was changed from the incandescent oil-vapor lamp to an electric incandescent lamp because commercial electricity

Fire Island's first-order Fresnel lens on display at the Franklin Institute in Philadelphia. *Courtesy of Fire Island National Seashore.*

lines had been brought to the station. A motor drive replaced the clockworks and weights that had made the lens revolve.[73]

The light station's first water supply and sewage system was installed in 1931, so the keepers and their families no longer had to rely on two wells. They also got bathrooms to replace the outhouses. The change was spurred by a letter two years earlier from the U.S. surgeon general to the commissioner of the Bureau of Lighthouses noting that a New York State Department of Health engineer had observed unsanitary conditions at the lighthouse, in part because "the privy was too close to the wells which supply drinking water."[74]

Among the first light tenders to benefit from the new plumbing was Adrien J. Boisvert, keeper from 1934 to 1941. He was thirty-three when he and his new wife, Alice, arrived on Fire Island. He was profiled in the *Sunday Island News* in 1935, with his last name misspelled.

The reporter described him as a "serious, rolly-polly lighthouse keeper" and "friendly little lighthouse boss." To pass his spare time, he relied on his "wife and an organ, made in Vermont, and a pack of cigarettes for each night he is on watch duty." The keeper also constructed models, including a miniature version of the station complete with foghorn made from an old alarm clock. Alice was described as a "sweet, shy feminine person."

Boisvert's first assistant keeper was Arthur Miller, who had been at Fire Island since 1928. His wife had been a munitions worker in World War I who survived a factory accident that cost her a kneecap and half a finger and damaged one eye. Their son Arthur Edward had died at age four in 1933, and his parents kept his ashes with them in a little casket rather than bury them because they never knew when Miller would be transferred to another lighthouse. Mrs. Miller, when not taking care of her other children, made beach plum wine that she served to visitors.[75]

Boisvert and his family had the harrowing experience of living

Adrien J. Boisvert was the keeper at Fire Island from 1934 to 1941. *Courtesy of Lighthouse Digest.*

Top: Assistant keeper Gus Axelson in the watch room of the Fire Island tower in 1934. *Courtesy of Lighthouse Digest.*

Middle: Assistant keeper Gus Axelson and his wife with child in the keeper's dwelling at Fire Island in 1934. *Courtesy of Lighthouse Digest.*

Below: The water rose almost to the terrace level during the famous Hurricane of 1938. *Courtesy of Fire Island National Seashore.*

through the Great Hurricane of 1938, which devastated much of eastern Long Island. It made landfall in the middle of Fire Island on September 21 with 121-mile-per-hour sustained winds. It destroyed structures all along Fire Island, including buildings and towers around the light station. But the brick lighthouse and dwelling survived unscathed.

The following year, the light station was electrified when a cable was laid along the bottom of the Great South Bay. The cable could be temperamental in bad weather, shorting out and leaving the keepers and their families dependent on lanterns and other old-fashioned devices.[76]

Even though the lighthouse service had been merged into the newly created Coast Guard in 1915, the men who tended the Fire Island Lighthouse continued to be called keepers until 1941. That year, Roy V. Wood, who took over as the head man in May, had the title of officer in charge. From then on, the keepers were all identified by their Coast Guard ranks.

Gottfried Mahler of Springfield Gardens, Queens, was officer in charge from 1948 to 1954. He enlisted in the Coast Guard on June 8, 1942, shortly after turning eighteen. He was inspired by the ships and work of the men in the service at the Atlantic Beach station near where he and his father had often fished when he was growing up. He was quartermaster on the buoy tender *Mangrove* and had other assignments. On December 16, 1945, he married Marilyn, whom he had met when he was a hall monitor at Andrew Jackson High School in Queens. After the couple had a son, Richard, Gottfried hoped for an assignment where he could live with family on Long Island. He was fortuitously appointed keeper at Fire Island in September 1948 when he was twenty-three and his wife twenty-one.

The entire time Mahler ran the station, his assistant was Robert W. Hodges, who lived with his wife, Edna, and their two sons. The two men found the dwelling hardly ready to accommodate families. During the war, it had housed up to fifty men in double-decked bunkbeds, and the space was worn and depressing with

Keeper Roy V. Wood served from 1938 to 1943. *Courtesy of Fire Island National Seashore.*

blackout curtains and battleship-gray floors. Marilyn bought rugs, curtains and furniture and put up wallpaper. Her washing machine made life somewhat easier, spinning most of the water out of the clothes so she could hang them out on the line to dry. In bad weather, the laundry would dry indoors on a six-foot-high wooden rack.

The dwelling was divided into two duplex apartments. Each had a living area and kitchen downstairs and two bedrooms upstairs. The first-floor central hall was a reception area. The restored dwelling now has a matched set of staircases leading up from the central hall, which was thought to be the original configuration. But when the Mahler and Hodges families were in residence, there was only one

Keeper Gottfried Mahler displays a fresh catch. *Courtesy of Fire Island Lighthouse Preservation Society.*

stairway, situated on the east side. The stairs led to an upstairs landing and a shared guestroom. There were spiral staircases connecting the first and second floors of each apartment. There were three bathrooms on the second floor.

Like their predecessors, Mahler or his assistant initially had to climb to the lantern room twice a day to switch the beam on and off and raise and lower the curtains. They had to tend to the backup electrical generators, polish the huge brass lamp and lens at least twice a week and clear away birds that smashed into the glass lantern at the top of the tower.

Mahler and Hodges no longer had to climb the tower morning and night after 1949, when the Fresnel lens and lamp that had been transferred from Shinnecock in 1933 were replaced by an automated Crouse-Hinds electric light. During the month it took for a crew of four engineers from the Staten Island depot to make the switch, the lighthouse was dark for ten days. The replacement light was actually two lights stacked on top of each other, each with one-thousand-watt halogen bulbs. That light, used for two decades, is on display in the keeper's dwelling visitor center. However, the Fire Island Lighthouse Preservation Society is seeking National Park Service approval to move it into the new lens building. When the old Fresnel lens was hoisted down the side of the tower with blocks and tackle and transported to Staten Island, it was badly damaged. Its fate is unknown.[77]

One of Mahler's most distinctive memories was the foggy night in April 1950 when the 432-foot freighter *Hurricane* ran up on the sandbar offshore. The ship's foghorn sounded so close that it rattled dishes in the keeper's dwelling and roused Mahler's sleeping family. The next morning, he saw the ship was just off the beach because of unusually high tides. The vessel remained mired in the sand for thirteen days, until two oceangoing tugs pulled it off.

When Marilyn Mahler was pregnant with her second child, the Coast Guard insisted she leave the island. She stayed with her parents in Elmont until she delivered her second son. When she returned to Fire Island, Helen Woodhull, wife of Ocean Beach School principal Richard Woodhull, organized a baby shower at her home. The Mahlers shared a great sense of humor, which they demonstrated in the birth announcement for Godfrey:

GOTTFRIED E. MAHLER, Quartermaster 1/c
U.S. COAST GUARD
MARILYN E. MAHLER, Housewife 1/c
CIVILIAN
Announce the launching of a new
Coast Guard Cut-up
The
GODFREY GORDON MAHLER
At Mercy Hospital, Rockville Centre, L.I.
On December 1, 1950 at 0830
Displacement—Pounds
Stem to Stern—18 Inches
Capacity to Hold—8 Ounces

SPECIAL FEATURES
1. Perpetually wet decks
2. Super-Strength fog horn
3. Shock-proof after bulkhead
4. Water-tight integrity—None!
5. Steering gear strictly unreliable

Will be anchored at home port after 12 December at Fire Island Light Station, Fire Island, NY.

Launching details handled by Dr. LaMariana
(Due to the present war shortage of materials, this model was launched bare
of all excess rigging.)

Results of trial run:
Smooth sailing.
Weathered all storms.
Weather forecast: WET!

Marilyn Mahler called the light station "a haven for a family." But she added that she and other keepers' wives needed to be skilled in switching on the emergency power when the electrical cable running under the bay from the South Shore failed. They also needed to be able to operate the radio-direction-finder beacon when their husbands weren't around. The family always left the door to the keeper's house unlocked in case a stranded boater needed shelter.

On the fiftieth anniversary of the Wright brothers' first flight, December 17, 1953, the lighthouse families received a visit from Flying Santa, aka author Edward Rowe Snow. He was one of several pilots who began delivering gifts to isolated lighthouses in the Northeast in 1929. Mahler was servicing the lens when a plane buzzed the tower. After the keeper descended, the plane made another pass and dropped a box with a parachute just west of the lighthouse. It landed near the dirt access road, nicknamed Burma Road after the World War II supply route in Asia. The box contained presents for the Mahler and Hodges families, including a flannel shirt for Gottfried, scarves for the wives, handmade wooden cars for the boys, candy, newspapers, coffee and a box of spices. The Flying Santa flight has been resurrected as a special event for children. The thirteenth reenactment in 2016 attracted a crowd of three hundred and a visit from Santa at the top of the tower. In May 1954, the Mahler family witnessed another flight, but this one took a tragic turn: a plane flown by a twenty-five-year-old Civil Air Patrol pilot crashed into the bay. The pilot later died at Southside Hospital in Bay Shore.

In 1954, with Marilyn pregnant again, two hurricanes, Carole and Edna, were headed to Long Island. She told her husband that she was worried about what would happen to their two young boys if the ocean threatened the keeper's dwelling. "We'll climb the tower—it has survived the Hurricane of '38 and all other weather for almost a hundred years," he replied. As he told a reporter years later: "Your job was to stay there and keep the light going. And besides, there was no place to go; the tide was up." The

Postcard view of the lighthouse. *Author's collection.*

storm surge rose to within six inches of the fieldstone terrace in front of the dwelling and tower but spared the structures.

Dwight, the third Mahler child, was also delivered in a South Shore hospital and not on the barrier island, although "we came close," Mahler joked. The shower for the infant, named for President Dwight D. Eisenhower, was also organized by Mrs. Woodhull, but this time at the light station.

Although there were no bridges connecting Fire Island with the rest of Long Island at the time, the family was not totally isolated. Mahler got around in Coast Guard vehicles, but Marilyn was not allowed to drive them as a civilian. So, in 1949, the couple traveled inland to Hicksville and purchased a 1931 Ford Model A for fifty dollars. It was towed to Bay Shore and loaded on a freight ferry for the trip across the bay. Marilyn drove it on errands and to meetings of her knitting club, the Knit-wits. To get across the bay, Mahler had a skiff with a twelve-horsepower engine. Because of the boat, his friends nicknamed him Captain Flat Bottom. He didn't care, as the craft allowed him to go island-hopping on days off to visit places like Bill Seuter's Bait Station on West Island. It also allowed trips to Ocean Beach to attend the Union Free Church. Relatives would come to the lighthouse to visit for a week in the summer, taking the ferry to Kismet, east of the lighthouse. Other island residents would visit them as well. When they had time off, they vacationed by visiting other Long Island lighthouses, including Montauk and Coney Island, and light stations along the New Jersey coast.

Gottfried Mahler was an accomplished gardener and grew vegetables and flowers on the west side of the lighthouse. On a dune north of the tower, he planted red and white cedar trees. During the Mahlers' time at Fire Island, lots of trash and other things washed up on the beach. Mahler and Hodges used some of the flotsam to build a walkway from the boathouse to the bay. One thing that almost washed up on the bay side was alive. When Richard was six and Godfrey two, they spotted a small dog struggling near the shore and rescued it. The boys wanted to keep the dachshund, but their father called the Coast Guard station and learned that the year-old dog had fallen overboard from a cabin cruiser owned by a Patchogue man. The pup stayed at the lighthouse for a week until the owner retrieved him. The boys did have other animals, however. In a wet spot near the artesian well, their father built a fishpond with cement and bricks left over from the original lighthouse and dwelling. It was stocked with goldfish and supported a resident population of ducks and geese. The family had two donated guinea hens to serve as watchdogs. And Mahler ordered two dozen chicks from Sears and ended up with an egg route through Saltaire and Fair Harbor.

Mahler left Fire Island in December 1954 when he was reassigned to the tender *Sassafras*, on which he had served before coming to Fire Island. He would later conduct hydrographic and plankton studies aboard the 255-foot cutter *Owasco*, on which he was quartermaster. He retired from the Coast Guard on July 1, 1962, and returned to Fire Island to work as a maintenance man for the Village of Saltaire. The Mahlers had a daughter, Roxanne, in 1963. The family moved to the other side of the bay in 1967 when Mahler took a job with the Brentwood School District, a position he retained until he retired in 1985.

The couple maintained their link to the lighthouse by volunteering as docents there. Mahler said he had always taken his job as keeper very seriously. "You have to realize that lives were at stake," he told a reporter in 1986. Gottfried Mahler died in 2012 and his wife two years later.[78]

Bob Hodges, who began at Fire Island in 1947 as an assistant, became officer in charge at the end of 1955 and remained in the job until the beginning of 1958. In an interview with National Park Service staff in 1985, Hodges talked about maintaining the light and the radio beacon. "The guy that had the duty was there for 24 hours, and turned the light on, the light off....He kept a constant watch on the radio beacon." The keepers were supposed to go up to the lantern room at dawn to shut off the lamp

Gottfried and Marilyn Mahler, pictured here in 2008, volunteered as docents at the lighthouse after Gottfried's retirement from the Coast Guard. *Courtesy of Joe Lachat.*

and cover the old Fresnel lens with curtains "because the sunshine could set the thing on fire. It really concentrated the rays." But they invented a remote control system so they could push a button on the ground to drop the curtain to protect the lens. The lighthouse inspectors were never the wiser. Hodges said the light only went out twice during his tenure, once during an electrical storm and another time when a part on the motor that rotated the lens broke.

Arnold A. Leiter was assigned to the lighthouse to serve under Hodges in early 1955. He complained that Hodges would often be doing personal work in surrounding communities while he and the other assistant had to handle all of the lighthouse chores. Once when Hodges complained that two assistants were not getting enough scraping, painting and other work accomplished, Leiter responded that they would have gotten more work done if the keeper had been there helping them. Hodges firmly reminded his subordinate of how the military chain of command worked, and presumably the assistant kept his complaints to himself in the future. Leiter remained in the position until December 12, 1959, when the records show he "died of heart attack while on liberty." In 1958, Hodges was transferred to the Montauk Point Light, where he remained until his retirement in the 1960s.[79]

The Coast Guard staff at the lighthouse starting in 1959 was officer in charge Gene L. Michaels and engineman third class Richard A. Lee. Their wives were featured in a February 13, 1961 *Newsday* story about life at the station. Jane Michaels, a mother of three, said she baked her own bread and cut the hair of family members. "I think we have closer family ties than most people," she said. "There's no church here in the winter and we give the children their Sunday school lessons. Every day June [Lee] and I bake something. This year, I preserved some wild beach plum jelly and we picked our own cranberries for Thanksgiving."

From the time the first lighthouse began operating in 1826, the only way to reach the site had been by boat or across the ice in winter. That changed on June 13, 1964, when the first bridge across the inlet was completed, connecting Fire Island with the rest of Long Island.[80]

With the light automated, the Coast Guard decided in 1969 that it no longer needed to have staff live at the lighthouse to maintain it. So Duane Butler and Warren Kelly were transferred, ending a line of keepers going back 143 years.[81]

But one thing never changed: maintenance of the brick tower continued to be a problem because of the harsh environment. By 1956, with the tower last painted in 1945, the structure had lost large portions of its exterior finish. A 1966 Coast Guard memo stated that "permanent repairs to the structure to prevent further deterioration and injury (or death) to personnel from falling stucco are required now." Permanent repairs were estimated to cost $120,000. Temporary repairs, "with no guarantee of permanence," would cost between $35,050 and $60,000. The report noted that the previous year, $11,500 had been spent on temporary exterior wall repairs, "which are already failing."[82]

The Coast Guard never made either temporary or permanent repairs. Instead, in the early 1970s, the service initiated plans to spend $120,000 to replace the lighthouse with a seventy-foot tower equipped with a searchlight optics system. That plan was scrapped when the Long Island State Park Commission began to build a water tower two miles to the west at Robert Moses State Park.

The Coast Guard made a historic announcement on March 17, 1972, revealing it would extinguish the lighthouse at the end of the following year after almost a century and a half of service. It would be replaced with an automatic beacon atop the state park water tower. The agency stated that there would be "only a minimal change in the light's flashing characteristics." Captain Thomas T. Wetmore, chief of the Coast Guard Third District

Aids to Navigation Branch, said the light would beam two powerful strobe-like flashes every ten seconds. The old light used a standard incandescent lightbulb and rotating lens combination that flashed once every seven and a half seconds. The new light would utilize sequential pulsing of light from flashtubes filled with xenon gas. The water tower light was the second of its kind in the seven states of the Third District after the Ambrose Light Tower marking the entrance to New York Harbor. Four flash tubes—two primary and two backups, activated automatically in case of malfunction—would be operated by solid-state circuitry monitored by a control panel at the nearby Fire Island Coast Guard Station. The agency noted the water tower was approximately thirty feet taller than the lighthouse, and on a clear night, the new light would be visible for more than twenty miles. It said the $61,000 cost of installing the new light would be substantially less than repairing the old light or building a new one somewhere else. The new apparatus would require minimal maintenance because it had no moving parts. For the immediate future, two Coast Guard families living at the lighthouse would remain there. Once they were relocated, the agency expected the property

The deteriorated tower and light station before the 1987 restoration. *Courtesy of* Lighthouse Digest.

would be turned over to the National Park Service for inclusion in Fire Island National Seashore.

The decision apparently had been made the previous May when the General Services Administration decided that eighty-one acres around the lighthouse would be declared surplus and offered to other federal agencies. The National Park Service obtained a one-year permit for the lighthouse tract, which bought time for Fire Island National Seashore officials to decide if they wanted the lighthouse permanently.

The Coast Guard extinguished the lighthouse at midnight on December 31, 1973, as planned. But thanks to a group of dedicated volunteers, it would not stay dark.[83]

8

THE RELIGHTING

S erving no practical purpose, the Fire Island Lighthouse continued to deteriorate.

Then, in 1978, Marilyn Roberts of Bay Shore read a newspaper article about plans to demolish the lighthouse as the Shinnecock tower had been three decades earlier. She showed the news story to her husband, banker Thomas F. Roberts III, and they agreed something should be done. They enlisted Norma Murray Ervin, president of the Fire Island Association, a residents' civic group, and the Fire Island Lighthouse Preservation Society began to take shape.[84]

The preservationists were heartened in 1978 when Congress approved legislation introduced by Representative James Grover to include the lighthouse tract in Fire Island National Seashore. Having the property managed by an agency whose mission included interpretation of history and historic preservation seemed to present an opportunity for keeping the lighthouse standing in perpetuity. With support from the preservationists, the Coast Guard transferred custody of 81.4 vacant acres to the park service on August 16, 1979. The Coast Guard turned over ownership of the remaining 37.2 acres, including all the structures, on April 10, 1981. But even the listing of the light station in the National Register of Historic Places on September 11, 1981, didn't guarantee its survival.[85]

The fears of Tom and Marilyn Roberts and the other preservationists were confirmed in 1981 when the Coast Guard declared the lighthouse unrepairable and slated it for demolition. Cognizant that the park service did not have the financial capability to restore and maintain the facility, the organizers of the lighthouse preservation society incorporated the nonprofit group in 1982 to restore the structures and get the Coast Guard to relight the tower.

The society secured the first agreement between a community fundraising organization and the park service to restore a historic site under the terms of the 1980 Historic Preservation Act. (The Statue of Liberty–Ellis Island project was the second.) On August 6, 1982, the national seashore superintendent and society president Tom Roberts signed cooperative agreements that would allow the organization's restoration project to proceed.

The painted covering flaking off the tower before the 1987 restoration. *Courtesy of* Lighthouse Digest.

"This effort is not directed to 'saving the lighthouse' just to save it," Roberts said. "It is directed to saving the lighthouse to put it to work, educating us with the lessons it holds, inspiring us with the heroics of its history, and linking us with a past that can fortify us for the future—all while it is restored to its historical and rightful place in providing safe navigation of our maritime craft." The group raised $50,000 for an architectural, engineering and historical study on rehabilitating the tower and turning the keeper's quarters into a visitor center.[86]

The study was completed by the park service in 1983. It documented that the tower's protective cement coating dating to 1912 was seriously deteriorated, with large sections breaking loose, probably because the bricks and their cement coating reacted differently to heat and cold. "The sheer weight of the concrete is pulling the coating completely away from the wall, exposing the brick surface of the 1858 tower." Some of the bricks exposed had fallen from the tower. There were large cracks in the lower white stripe and numerous small cracks in the upper black stripe. "The interior of the tower is plagued by high humidity levels, broken windows, and clogged ventilation and drainage cavities, resulting in extensive chipping of the painted finishes, efflorescence of the brick work, and corrosion of the metalwork." The walls of the rooms at the top of the tower were showing severe cracking.

The report pointed out that any effort to restore the keeper's dwelling would have to deal with significant architectural changes over the years. At the time of the report, the building was the home for two park service employees and their families. It had been divided into two apartments in a 1961 modernization. Those changes "alter the structure's interior more drastically in plan and architectural detail than at any other time in its history." Outside, "the terrace is in poor condition. The paving is loose and provides an uneven and dangerous walking surface. The embankment walls are covered with overgrowth, and plagued with cracks and deteriorated mortar joints."

The report said that restoring the buildings to their 1858 appearance "would require a substantial amount of restoration." And even if the society wanted to do that, "there is not enough information to guide such work, and even if there were, it would mean the removal of many layers of history." In 1858, the cement coating was painted a yellow cream color rather than the black and white stripes and the balcony railings were different from those in the modern era, the report noted. The keeper's quarters had a slate roof rather than modern asphalt shingles, and the doors and windows were different. There were now two chimneys rather than the original four.

Another option, restoring the tower to its 1973 appearance at the end of its service life, "would require only minimal restoration work. However, the proposed plan is to adaptively reuse the interiors of the structures for educational museum purposes. It would be desirable to have the covered passageway extant, and all the doors and windows [covered over in the past] open for this use." When the lighthouse was built, a covered passageway connected it to the keeper's quarters. The passageway was removed around 1950 and replaced by a vestibule in 1961.

Because of the complications of the first two options, the park service recommended restoring the buildings to their appearance in 1939—the year the Coast Guard took over the lighthouse service and the beacon was electrified. "The covered passageway could be rebuilt, and all the doorways and windows brought back to full use. Only limited restoration would be prescribed." That was the plan adopted.[87]

The agency's 1984 estimate for restoration of the light station to its 1939 appearance totaled $707,972. That broke down to $539,398 to restore the tower, with the biggest part of that expense being $170,800 to remove the peeling three-inch-thick concrete skin. Exterior restoration

The kitchen of the keeper's dwelling before the 1986 restoration of the building. *Courtesy of Fire Island National Seashore.*

of the keeper's dwelling was estimated at $94,764. Reconstruction of the missing covered passageway between the dwelling and the tower was estimated at $73,810.[88]

The park service report encouraged restoration because "the history of the Fire Island lighthouses intricately reflects the history of the lighthouse system....The erection of both lighthouses, the first in 1825–1826 and the second in 1858–1859, occurred during significant periods of lighthouse expansion and reorganization."

The significant projected costs did not daunt the society. Based on the park service estimates, the preservation group decided its initial fundraising goal should be $1.1 million to restore the dwelling inside and out as a visitor center and museum. It also decided it should set a deadline of raising that money within two years, by December 1984, according to a history of the society. The first year was spent primarily organizing and incorporating as a nonprofit. The group established its headquarters in donated space in the Fire Island Ferries Terminal and furnished it with donated furniture and office equipment. The society's board—which included attorneys, historians and businessmen—was augmented by creating an advisory council of forty prominent Long Islanders headed by fashion designer Liz Claiborne.

Two Fire Island residents—Claiborne and Norma Murray Ervin—helped launch the fundraising campaign by donating more than $100,000 and then repeated the gift in 1984. By May 1984, donations—from more than five thousand individuals—had surpassed $660,000. The majority of the donors were descendants of immigrants for whom the lighthouse had been their first sight of America.

In 1984, Congressman Thomas Downey, buoyed by the society's fundraising efforts, persuaded Congress to allocate $2 million to the park service to aid the lighthouse project. This paid for rehabilitation of the keeper's quarters, restoration of the site surrounding the lighthouse, construction of boardwalks and renovating an old annex building into housing and offices for park rangers.

By 1986, the society had raised $1.2 million to turn the rehabilitated dwelling into a visitor center and museum, and the Coast Guard paid for installation of a new lighting apparatus in the tower. The stage was set for bringing the light station back to life.

Sunday, May 25, 1986, was the big day. After two years of rehabilitation, the visitor center in the keeper's quarters was dedicated early in the evening in honor of Norma Ervin, who had died before the project's completion. A letter of congratulations from President Ronald Reagan was read: "Nancy and I are proud that the Fire Island Light shines again, as an aid to navigation and as an historic link to our nautical past." Guests marveled at the restored 1949 Crouse-Hinds electric light apparatus displayed on the first floor. But the keeper's quarters would not be open regularly to the public until the next year.

From left to right: Congressman Thomas Downey, Fire Island Lighthouse Preservation Society president Thomas Roberts III, former Fire Island National Seashore superintendent Jack Hauptman and Coast Guard lieutenant Rodney Bowles signing paperwork to allow restoration of the light station buildings. *Courtesy of Fire Island National Seashore.*

After the sun set, the focus shifted to the tower. A Relighting Regatta, billed as the largest flotilla of boats ever assembled on Long Island, was on hand to watch from the Great South Bay.

A boat parade was led by a 116-year-old tugboat, *Charlotte*, and the seventy-foot schooner *Commodore*, built in 1913. More than one hundred musicians of the New Image Drum and Bugle Corps played on the vessel *Vagabond*, with the activities simulcast over a local radio station. Aboard the flotilla flagship, the charter boat *Evening Star*, fourteen-year-old Peter J. Nappi of Hauppauge, Long Island, great-great-great-great-grandson of keeper Eliphalet Smith, joined Roberts and preservation society historian Henry R. Bang at a ceremonial switch. "Finally, we have our light back," Roberts said. A *Newsday* reporter described what came next: "At 8:59 p.m., floodlights illuminating the tower were extinguished. Aboard the boat *Evening Star*, people began counting down until, precisely at 9 p.m. a ceremonial switch was thrown." (The relighting was actually done by park service personnel at the lighthouse after they got a radio call from *Evening Star*.) "The light came on, first tentatively as a flicker, and then, in full force. The double white rotating beam atop the 168-foot tower, visible for 24 miles, began a slow rotation, flashing its warning and welcome out into the Atlantic every 7.5 seconds. Boats blew their horns, people cheered, the band played and some people on boats set off flares and fireworks."

Karen Thynne, eighteen, of Farmingdale, who was watching from a nearby dock with her brother, Gary, twenty-six, said, "I love it. As a native Long Islander, I wouldn't have missed it. I feel real patriotic." Liz Claiborne said, "Like the Statue of Liberty was always the symbol of the U.S., this was always a symbol of Fire Island." The navigation light atop the state park water tower was extinguished, and the society had the satisfaction of again seeing the lighthouse on government nautical charts as an official aid to navigation.[89]

But the organization's work was not done. It needed to raise another $300,000 to complete the restoration of the tower because costs had increased since the first estimate, primarily from inflation. By the following year, the society had raised an additional $500,000, allowing what would become a two-year project to move forward.

The deteriorated exterior stucco was replaced with a sprayed-on coating of reinforced cement topped by a waterproof coating painted with the familiar black and white stripes. "This has been the most visible phase of our effort," Roberts explained. "Actually many people thought that restoring the tower should have been our first priority, simply because it was most obviously in need of repair. It was important to pursue the sequence we planned in order to have a place for visitors to learn about our efforts and about the history of the lighthouse—why it was important to save it." He added that having the keeper's dwelling restored first provided a staging area and temporary home for the owners of Jan A. Blanck Company, the contractor restoring the tower. Blanck specialized in applying Shotcrete, the concrete coating sprayed on the tower in August and September. "This coating was tested and the results were even stronger than engineers had first predicted," said Walter Sedovic, the historical architect overseeing the project for the U.S. Department of the Interior.

Blanck and his wife, Siv, fell in love with the lighthouse. They had previously worked on mineshaft and tunnel projects in Hong Kong, Africa and throughout Europe and the United States, but the lighthouse was special. "The lighthouse is a romantic landmark, and one cannot help but feel a part of its history while working on it," Siv Blanck said. "In addition it is a beautifully proportioned structure. We wanted to make it look as perfect as possible." The couple lived on the second floor of the keeper's dwelling and enjoyed watching the change of seasons on the barrier beach. "The birds and the deer, the different kinds of things that grow have been an endless source of pleasure," she said. Reluctant to leave, the couple was pleased when they were asked to restore the inside of the tower and the staircase as well. The interior walls were air-blasted to remove dirt and flaking paint and then left unpainted. The steps that could be removed were taken outside for sandblasting and then finished with two coats of primer and one coat of black enamel. The other stairs were treated in place.

In October, the black and white stripes were reapplied with an acrylic emulsion paint designed to protect the concrete from moisture. The first strokes were applied by board members and advisors to the project. The last steps were installing new bronze porthole windows into the watch room of the tower before the arched landing windows were restored and reinstalled, making the tower watertight. One unexpected discovery during the tower work was that a family of barn owls had made a nest under the gallery. Park ranger Allan O'Connell had to go up the scaffolding to remove the babies, which he said looked about ready to be on their way anyway. They were transported to ornithologists at the Jamaica Bay Wildlife Refuge, where they were adopted by another mother owl.

In 1987, with its focus shifting from fundraising and restoration to operation and programming, the society became a membership organization. It now has more than three hundred members.

The success of the society's fundraising campaign inspired other nonprofit organizations to begin restoration projects at other Long Island lighthouses, including the Lloyd Harbor and Montauk Point beacons.

At Fire Island, the biggest payoff for the society's years of hard work finally arrived in 1989. On August 7—National Lighthouse Day—after two years of rehabilitation of the structure, the tower was opened to visitors for the first time.[90]

9

RETURN OF THE FRESNEL LENS

W hile elated at completion of the tower restoration in 1989, the Fire Island Lighthouse Preservation Society and historians were troubled that something crucial was still missing from the site: the original first-order Fresnel lens.

That unique artifact installed in the second tower when it was built in 1858 had been loaned by the Coast Guard to the Franklin Institute in 1933 after seventy-five years of service. The preservation society and the National Park Service wanted it back and began discussions with the Philadelphia museum. Serious negotiations began in 1997. But it would take another decade to bring it home.

In the meantime, the preservation society had lots of other work to do. To extend the hours the tower was open for public tours, in 1989 the organization began paying salaries of park rangers assigned to staff the station.

After all the progress on restoration and interpretation, the society suffered a setback. In December 1991, a water line for the fire sprinkler system in the keeper's dwelling burst, flooding the exhibit rooms. Faced with the unexpected cost of cleanup and restoring what had already been restored, the society decided it could no longer afford to pay for staffing and other operating costs while continuing to restore and preserve the property. So it reduced the number of days the structures were open, and educational programs were greatly curtailed.

The society was buoyed, however, in 1992 when Congress appropriated $545,000 for capital projects. The covered passageway between the tower and dwelling removed in the 1950s was reconstructed, the uneven stone terrace around the dwelling was repaired and the remaining foundation of the 1826 lighthouse had been stabilized by 1993. The next year, the society paid $25,000 to reset the terrace stones after the initial work done by the park service contractor proved to be faulty. When the tower needed to be repointed and repainted in 1995, the society added $35,000 to the park service's $30,000 allocation.[91]

With the preservation society already carrying so much of the burden for maintaining the light station, the organization took a major step in 1996. After a year of negotiations, it signed a "cooperating association agreement" with the park service that transferred responsibility for all daily operations and routine maintenance to the society. The ten-year agreement for the buildings and about half an acre of property stipulated that the preservation group would pay for operating costs, estimated to be $200,000 a year. The park service would continue to pay for structural repairs, and the Coast Guard would still maintain the light apparatus. Fire Island became the fifth lighthouse on Long Island to be operated by a nonprofit group.

The society said the agreement would allow the lighthouse to be open more frequently. "We have school groups who want to get in but can't because we hadn't had the authority to put more staff there," society president Gayle Haines said. She added that exhibits could be expanded and improved because "we can do a lot more with less if we're privatized." David Luchsinger, chief of administration at Fire Island National Seashore, added, "We have never been funded to operate the lighthouse. Because of the budget constraints, this appears to be the ideal situation for both parties."[92]

The society took advantage of its increased control in 1997 to renovate part of the basement in the keeper's quarters as a classroom. Visitation that year reached forty thousand. In 1998, the hours of operation increased, with the lighthouse and visitor center open seven days a week during the spring-to-fall season and school group tours expanded to five days per week.

As the twentieth century was coming to a close, there was a development in Philadelphia that would give the preservation society and park service something they had wanted for two decades. The 1858 Fresnel lens that the Coast Guard loaned to the Franklin Institute in 1933 had gone on display prominently in the museum's Hall of Science when it opened the following New Year's Day. But as the museum began a multiyear major renovation project, it decided in 2000 that the lens, which had no connection to Philadelphia, did not fit into its planned exhibitions. So the components

A convoy carrying twenty-one crates containing the nine hundred pieces of the Fresnel lens arrives back on Fire Island in 2007 after the artifact spent seventy-four years in Philadelphia. *Courtesy of Joe Lachat.*

of the four-ton relic were placed into thirty-four crates and stored in a Philadelphia warehouse at the preservation society's expense.

In 1997, after two years of informal discussions, the park service and preservation society officially kicked off an effort to get the lens back with a written request to the institute. Their concept was to display it at a Fire Island National Seashore visitor center planned for Patchogue or a new building at the light station. Putting the lens back into the tower was deemed impossible because of the cost and the need to have a modern optic in place. And if the Fresnel were reinstalled in the lantern room, the public would not be able to see it because the steep ladder leading up from the watch room and the tight confines of the lantern room made it likely that the lens or a visitor might be injured.

Once the lens had been removed from the museum, the park service and preservation society stepped up their efforts. Constantine Dillon, superintendent of Fire Island National Seashore, said, "We would very much like to have it back at Fire Island National Seashore where it came from. Interpreting the maritime history of the Great South Bay and the Atlantic Ocean off Fire Island is a big part of what we want to do. At the present time we don't have any place to display it." But he wanted it to be the centerpiece of a new $4.5 million visitor center in Patchogue if the money could be found to construct it.

The preservation society, however, wanted the lens back at the light station. Tom Roberts, again serving as president, said, "We don't have space for it at the lighthouse but at some point in time we would like to see a visitor center built at the lighthouse and the building could be designed to house the lens."

There was no immediate decision by the Coast Guard on the disposition of the lens. At the time, there were only thirty-one first-order Fresnel lenses remaining around the country, and the agency valued them at between $900,000 and $1.5 million each, depending on their condition.[93]

As the new century began, the preservation society and the state parks department obtained a $250,000 grant from the New York legislature to build a boardwalk from the parking area at Robert Moses State Park Field 5 to the Fire Island National Seashore boundary. It would link up with the boardwalk already in place from the boundary to the lighthouse. The society also began restoring the boathouse at a cost of $10,000.

In 2001, visitation at the lighthouse exceeded 100,000 for the first time. The following year, the park service renovated the second floor of the keeper's quarters to install exhibits. And in 2003, the lighthouse was open year round for the first time. The boathouse rehabilitation was completed and the first displays installed. National Park Service director Fran Mainella participated in the dedication ceremony. All of the displays would be in place by 2007.[94]

In 2005, the Coast Guard announced it planned to replace the two-decade-old lighting apparatus with a more efficient system. The twin twenty-four-inch rotating airport-style beacon lights would be replaced with a single smaller strobe-type light that would not rotate and not be visible as far away as the existing light's twenty-three-mile range. Changing the light

The base of the Fresnel lens is unloaded on Fire Island. *Courtesy of Joe Lachat.*

apparatus would alter how the tower appeared to observers. And that was not welcome news for the lighthouse society after all the work and money it had put into restoration. Negotiations led to a compromise. In January 2006, the society and park service signed an extension of the cooperating association agreement for ten years. The society assumed responsibility for maintaining the light apparatus from the Coast Guard, which then classified the lighthouse as a private aid to navigation.

Maintaining the lighting apparatus and the backup generator in the basement of the keeper's dwelling meant assuming an estimated $8,000 annual expense. But Roberts felt it was worth the money. "The main issue was to maintain the historical characteristic of the light, which was the sweeping beam," he said. He noted that when the Coast Guard installed one of the stationary Vega lights in the Montauk Point Lighthouse, preservationists and mariners complained about its appearance and reduced visibility. Chief Boatswain's Mate Anthony Certa, head of the Coast Guard aids to navigation team for Long Island, said the agency decided to give the lighting system to the preservation society because "they are very well organized and established and they have been maintaining the structure." He explained that the Vega light is "a modern piece of equipment that we can get parts for. With the lantern that's in the Fire Island Lighthouse, they actually have to make parts for it when something breaks. It's very expensive to run and it wasn't going to be efficient for the Coast Guard any longer. There would have been cost savings with the Vega lantern but it's not as aesthetically pleasing as the older, wider beam." So the Coast Guard agreed to turn over at no cost the lighting equipment, including switching apparatus and some spare parts. Each light fixture was equipped with a backup one-thousand-watt bulb ready to take its place automatically when it burned out. The society organized a group of volunteers who were all engineering graduates of the State University of New York Maritime College in the Bronx, and they were trained to maintain the light by the Coast Guard.

Meanwhile, the park service's proposal to display the Fresnel lens in a new visitor center in Patchogue had stalled for lack of funding. Since the preservation society had always felt the artifact should be displayed on Fire Island, it began planning for a building to house the lens there. The concept was to build a replica of the demolished powerhouse, which had been erected west of the tower in 1895, on the original foundation. The park service had changed its policy in the 1980s and generally no longer approved re-creation of demolished buildings at historic sites. But the agency's regional office

The foundation of the old, and never used, power plant, which was chosen as the site for the new building to display the Fresnel lens. *Courtesy of Joe Lachat.*

encouraged the society to develop a plan, and the organization prepared an environmental assessment.

When the powerhouse had been demolished in the 1950s, the boathouse had been relocated onto its foundation. The society wanted to move the boathouse back to its original location by the bay. So, the project "will do two things," said society vice president Bob LaRosa. "It will give us a building big enough for the Fresnel lens and will restore the historic landscape." The exterior would resemble the 1895 building with a curved zinc metal roof and clerestory, or raised section running down the center, while the interior would be a climate-controlled display space of modern design. There were no architectural plans in existence for the powerhouse, but photographs were available showing it from all four sides, which would aid in its reconstruction. With no existing images of the interior, the society would have a blank canvas for its displays.

At the time, according to the U.S. Lighthouse Society, there were other first-order Fresnel lenses on display. Some were still in lantern rooms of lighthouses; some were operational and some not. Those on display included Seguin Island, Maine, and Saint Augustine, Florida, both still in use in the towers.[95]

The society's initiative to provide a home for the lens received a huge boost in 2006 when the organization received a $400,000 grant from New York State. The lens returned to Long Island for the first time since 1933 in

The lens building under construction in 2010. *Courtesy of Patti Stanton.*

March 2007. Its nine hundred pieces were taken to the Fire Island National Seashore curatorial center in Mastic Beach, awaiting a final decision by the park service on how best to display it. The preservation society paid for the move. The park service commissioned a study to evaluate the society's plan, which the organization estimated would cost $500,000, including the cost of restoring and reassembling the lens. Michael Reynolds, the new national seashore superintendent, said he and his staff now supported the society's plan "because it balances historic preservation with the best way for visitors to appreciate the light. It brings back an element that was missing—the old building that was originally on the site. It will be a low-key element on the site, but make a huge difference to visitors. They will be able to see the whole picture of what the original light was and see a piece of American heritage—the Fresnel lens that lighted lighthouses like this across the country and there are so few of them left." Before the year was out, the park service had given final approval to putting the lens in the reconstructed powerhouse, and the preservation society had a set of preliminary architectural plans.[96]

The society paid to relocate the boathouse to its original site in 2009. In January of that year, the ninety-acre light station site was designated a national historic district in the National Register of Historic Places.[97]

Construction of the 1,500-square-foot lens building began in July 2010 with completion anticipated by the following Memorial Day, the twenty-fifth anniversary of the relighting. The new building was erected above—but not on—the existing concrete powerhouse foundation. "We're not building

An oil can used by the keepers at Fire Island now in the archives of Fire Island National Seashore. *Photo by the author.*

on the slab; we are actually suspending it because it's historic and it wouldn't hold the weight of this building," Roberts explained.

The cedar-covered building was built by contractor Kenneth Herman of Oak Beach, a former society board member who volunteered his time to manage the $560,000 project paid for by the preservation society. The cost was also reduced because construction unions provided volunteer labor and twenty-seven vendors donated materials, saving the society more than $900,000.

The $358,448 park service contract for restoration and reassembly of the lens was awarded to MACTECH Engineering and Consulting of Kennesaw, Georgia. "There's quite a bit of restoration needed for the lens," Roberts said. "It really suffered through its years of being displayed at the Franklin Institute because of heat damage."

The team of five restoration specialists brought in by MACTECH was headed by "lampist" James Woodward, a forty-year Coast Guard veteran who after retiring founded an Arizona-based firm, The Lighthouse Consultant LLC. The team spent a month cleaning and repairing the parts of the lens at a national seashore building near the lighthouse.

The twenty-four glass panels made by the Henry Lepaute Company of Paris were rehabilitated by replacing deteriorated glazing compound and applying an acrylic compound to seal the components. Woodward found that five of the prisms were cracked all the way through, so he repaired them the same way the U.S. Lighthouse Service did in the early 1900s: with putty covered by a wrapping of brass in what is called a "lampist's repair." Many chips on the outer edges of the prisms were left as they were found intentionally. "That's the history of the lens," Woodward explained. "That's part of the story. You wouldn't want to repair it from a historic preservation point of view."

Then came the delicate two-week process of reassembling the Fresnel artifact in the display building, with International Chimney handling the rigging work. The lens prisms were removed from their custom-made foam-

A pennant that flew at the lighthouse now in the Fire Island National Seashore archives. *Photo by the author.*

padded packing crates and cleaned with a feather duster. Any glazing putty visible on their edges was covered with brown paint. The glass sections were lifted carefully into place with a block and tackle. Then they were fastened to the brass frame of the lens.

After one large bull's-eye prism was successfully mounted, Woodward exhaled and said, "After forty-five years I still shake when I do that." He had plenty of experience with lenses in those forty-five years, having restored more than two hundred of them, including about twenty first-order Fresnel relics. He had dismantled the Fire Island lens at the Franklin Institute in 2000.

A new electric motor was installed on the Fire Island lens to allow it to rotate in its new home. A one-hundred-watt light bulb was placed inside to illuminate it, spreading geometric shadows across the walls.[98]

Erecting the Fresnel lens building took longer than anticipated. It was not dedicated until July 22, 2011. By the end of the year, more than twenty-two thousand people had visited it.[99]

Two years later, the preservation society suffered a setback far more severe than the 1991 sprinkler system water pipe break. When Superstorm

Left: Rehabilitation of the lantern in 2013. *Photo by Anneliese Scheef, Lighthouse Digest archives.*

Below: A bosun's chair used to paint the tower now in the Fire Island National Seashore archives. *Photo by the author.*

Sandy crashed into the South Shore of Long Island on October 29, 2012, with eighty-mile-per-hour winds and record storm surges, the ocean washed across Fire Island into the bay and caused widespread damage at and around the light station. The basement of the keeper's dwelling flooded, and everything on the floor was ruined. All of the boardwalks around the complex except the one leading to the bay were washed away. It took almost a year for the society and National Park Service to repair all the damage at the complex and get it back into full operation. The park service boardwalk connecting it with Robert Moses State Park was not rebuilt until March 2014.[100]

Since the Fire Island Lighthouse Preservation Society was incorporated in 1982, $3.5 million has been spent on the light station structures. That includes $1.5 million raised by the society to restore the tower and keeper's dwelling, $1.6 million collected by the organization to build the lens building and about $400,000 from the federal government to restore the lens.

The preservation society continues to operate the light station complex under its cooperating association agreement with the National Park Service, which was renewed in January 2017 for another five years. With an annual budget of approximately $300,000, the organization now employs 3 full-time and 5 part-time seasonal employees, augmented by more than 140 volunteers.

Silverware used by the family of keeper George Thomas in the early 1900s in the Fire Island National Seashore archives. *Photo by the author.*

Going forward, the society is working with the park service to bring back lighthouse artifacts currently stored at the Fire Island National Seashore archives center at the William Floyd Estate in Mastic Beach. These include a U.S. Lighthouse Service pennant flown on Fire Island, an oil can used to carry lamp oil up the tower, a bosun's chair used to paint the tower and silverware used by the family of keeper George Thomas in the early 1900s. The transfer, which is pending approval from park service officials, is contingent on having proper display space for the artifacts. To provide that, the society received a pledge from a donor to cover the cost of a climate-controlled display cabinet for the keeper's dwelling.

The society also hopes the park service will approve its plan to relocate the 1949 Crouse-Hinds electric light apparatus now displayed on the first floor of the visitors' center to the new lens building so it can be viewed with the 1858 first-order Fresnel lens.

The organization also plans to restore one room on the second floor of the dwelling now used for exhibits to its historic appearance as a keeper's bedroom. Another goal is to build a deck behind the boathouse to provide a better view of the Great South Bay. The society also hopes to refurbish the service room, which is two floors below the lantern room in the tower, with furniture and artifacts to show how it would have looked when keepers spent the night there.

These projects are all part of the society's mission, which its president, Bob LaRosa, describes as "preserving this American historic treasure so people can enjoy learning about our local maritime heritage."

"The Fire Island Lighthouse Preservation Society has been instrumental in preserving the lighthouse and educating visitors for more than thirty years," Executive Director Dave Griese added. "With the National Park Service as a partner and the passion of our board, staff and volunteers, we expect to keep the light shining."

To plan a visit or for more information, go to
http://www.fireislandlighthouse.com or call (631) 661-4876.

APPENDIX A

LIGHTHOUSE STATION TIMELINE

1825–26   First lighthouse constructed.

1857–58   Second lighthouse constructed.

1891   Black and white bands, or "daymarks," painted on tower.

1895   Powerhouse constructed to provide electricity but never used. Building demolished in 1956.

1907   Incandescent oil vapor lamp installed.

1931   Major renovation of keeper's dwelling includes running water and first bathrooms. Outside privy demolished.

1933   The 1858 first-order Fresnel lens removed and loaned to Franklin Institute in Philadelphia. Replaced by simpler first-order Fresnel lens from demolished Shinnecock Lighthouse.

1938–39   Incandescent oil vapor lamp replaced with electric incandescent lamp.

1949   Crouse-Hinds electrified lighting apparatus installed.

1973   Coast Guard extinguishes light at midnight on December 31.

1978   Fire Island Lighthouse Preservation Society formed.

1981   Lighthouse declared "unsafe and beyond repair" by Coast Guard and slated for demolition.

1982   Fire Island Lighthouse Preservation Society is incorporated to raise funds to restore light station. Coast Guard cedes control of lighthouse tract and responsibility for lighthouse maintenance to National Park Service. Society signs agreement with Fire Island National Seashore to help rehabilitation and preservation of the lighthouse under the 1980 Preservation of Historic Structures Act.

1983   Coast Guard turns lighthouse property over to National Park Service.

1986   After four years and the raising of more than $1.5 million by the Fire Island Lighthouse Preservation Society, the organization and the National Park Service relight the tower with a revolving aero-beacon on May 25.

1987   The visitor center in the keeper's quarters opens.

1989   Light tower opened for public visitation for the first time.

1996   Operating agreement is signed with National Park Service to transfer daily operations and maintenance to society.

2000   Franklin Institute removes Fresnel lens from display and places it in a warehouse.

2006   Rotating beacon atop lighthouse is turned over to the preservation society by Coast Guard and classified as private aid to navigation.

2007   The 1858 Fresnel lens returns to Long Island.

2009   Boathouse is relocated to its historic position by the bay.

2010   Fresnel lens building construction begins.

2011   Fresnel lens building is dedicated on July 22.

2013   Superstorm Sandy floods keeper's quarters basement and destroys boardwalks, requiring nearly a year's efforts to resume normal operations.[101]

APPENDIX B

KEEPERS AND THEIR ASSISTANTS

Dates	Name	Title
1827–1835	? Isaacs	Keeper
05/17/1835–1844	Felix Dominy	Keeper
01/15/1844–1849	Eliphalet Smith	Keeper
01/19/1849–1849	John A. Hicks	Keeper
07/14/1849–1853	Selah Strong	Keeper
04/29/1850–1853	Benjamin Smith	First Assistant
1853–1859	Willet Smith	First Assistant
05/29/1853–04/12/1861	Benjamin Smith	Keeper
1859–1862	Stephen Fordham	First Assistant
03/19/1859–?	Samuel M. Smith	Second Assistant
1861–1864	J.J. Squires	Second Assistant
04/12/1861–01/19/1864	C.W. Fordham	Keeper
04/21/1862–05/26/1865	David Baldwin	Second Assistant
11/14/1862–03/29/1864	Stephen Griffin	First Assistant
03/28/1864–03/02/1869	Richard Eldridge	Assistant
03/29/1864–10/18/1864	Frank Wright	First Assistant
10/18/1864–11/11/1865	Aaron Burr	First Assistant

Dates	Name	Title
05/26/1865–05/04/1869	J.E. Hulse	Keeper
11/11/1865–06/05/1869	David S. Baldwin	Assistant
03/02/1869–06/05/1869	Edward Hulse	Assistant
05/04/1869–07/19/1870	Perry S. Wicks	Keeper
06/04/1869–09/13/1869	Hampton Sands	Assistant
06/05/1869–03/23/1870	Seth R. Hubbard	Assistant
06/05/1869–06/05/1869	Thomas Thorne	Assistant
09/13/1869–03/25/1870	Thomas Hawkins	Assistant
03/23/1870–06/23/1871	Charles Brown	Assistant
03/25/1870–07/06/1870	Luther Ketcham	Assistant
07/06/1870–07/23/1870	Uriah Brown	Assistant
07/28/1870–12/?/1871	Henry C. French	Keeper
08/24/1870–08/08/1871	Edwin Ruland	Assistant
06/23/1871–10/11/1871	Joseph Haynes	Assistant
08/08/1871–10/23/1872	Hugh Walsh	Assistant
10/11/1871–10/12/1872	Charles Brown	Assistant
12/18/1871–10/12/1872	Warren F. Clock	Keeper
11/30/1872–04/30/1873	William J. Bailey	Second Assistant
12/10/1872–08/16/1873	John Burke	First Assistant
01/02/1873–03/24/1874	Hugh Walsh	Keeper
04/30/1873–08/25/1873	Seth R. Hubbard	Second Assistant
08/25/1873–04/?/1874	Seth R. Hubbard	First Assistant
08/28/1873–08/28/1873	Timothy Terry	Second Assistant
10/09/1873–04/15/1874	John S. Jayne	Second Assistant
04/24/1874–12/02/1881	Seth R. Hubbard	Keeper
04/25/1874–05/05/1875	John S. Jayne	First Assistant
04/25/1874–05/05/1875	A.D. Buckley	Second Assistant
05/05/1875–10/05/1875	A.D. Buckley	First Assistant
05/05/1875–10/05/1875	Lorenzo D. Smith	Second Assistant

DATES	NAME	TITLE
10/05/1875–10/05/1876	Lorenzo D. Smith	First Assistant
10/05/1875–05/?/1876	Hubert Ruland	Second Assistant
05/20/1876–03/?/1878	Francis Box	Second Assistant
10/05/1876–04/23/1880	Lorenzo D. Smith	First Assistant
03/28/1878–10/21/1879	William H. Terry	Second Assistant
10/21/1879–04/23/1880	C.A. Blydenburg	Second Assistant
04/23/1880–05/24/1880	John Deery	First Assistant
05/24/1880–07/10/1883	C.A. Blydenburg	First Assistant
05/24/1880–10/03/1882	William A. Valentine	Second Assistant
12/02/1881–11/06/1886	Seth R. Hubbard	Keeper
10/03/1882–12/16/1882	James McDonald	Second Assistant
01/02/1883–06/04/1883	Francis Box	Second Assistant
07/02/1883–07/10/1883	George E. Abrams	Second Assistant
07/10/1883–05/22/1884	George E. Abrams	First Assistant
07/30/1883–08/21/1883	Charles Staats	Second Assistant
09/22/1883–07/22/1884	Epenetus C. Smith	Second Assistant
09/12/1884–09/26/1884	Walter B. Abrams	Second Assistant
09/26/1884–11/06/1885	Walter B. Abrams	First Assistant
02/21/1885–03/19/1885	Charles E. White	Second Assistant
04/02/1885–07/13/1885	George W. Ruland	Second Assistant
12/05/1885–04/27/1886	Sherman Pearsall	Second Assistant
04/27/1886–07/20/1886	David W. Anderson	Second Assistant
09/21/1886–11/06/1886	Nicholas O. Kortwright	Second Assistant
11/06/1886–07/23/1888	Charles F. Smith	Keeper
11/06/1886–05/03/1887	Nicholas O. Kortwright	First Assistant
11/06/1886–05/09/1887	Edward J. Udall	Second Assistant
05/09/1887–07/23/1888	Edward J. Udall	First Assistant
05/09/1887–04/01/1888	George Jayne	Second Assistant
04/04/1888–07/23/1888	John G. Skipworth	Second Assistant

Dates	Name	Title
07/23/1888–10/?/1909	Ezra S. Mott	Keeper
07/23/1888–01/02/1889	John G. Skipworth	First Assistant
08/14/1888–05/01/1890	David Williams	Second Assistant
01/02/1889–05/01/1890	John G. Skipworth	Second Assistant
03/29/1890–05/11/1892	David Williams	First Assistant
04/22/1890–06/19/1890	Joseph C. Wright	Second Assistant
06/19/1890–04/12/1892	Howard Poe	Second Assistant
04/09/1892–09/?/1901	Howard Poe	First Assistant
05/04/1892–04/01/1895	William H.H. Lake	Second Assistant
03/03/1895–04/04/1895	Uriah L. Brown	Second Assistant
04/11/1895–09/15/1895	Adolph Ott	Second Assistant
09/16/1895–08/10/1896	William H.H. Lake	Second Assistant
08/21/1896–09/?/1901	William H.H. Lake Jr.	Second Assistant
09/25/1901–05/18/1908	William H.H. Lake Jr.	First Assistant
10/08/1901–10/?/1903	Theodore M. Brower	Second Assistant
05/21/1907–06/23/1908	John Morgan	Second Assistant
11/02/1907–06/?/1908	Henry Burkhardt	Second Assistant
05/19/1908–04/?/1909	Henry Burkhardt	First Assistant
06/03/1908–10/?/1908	Walter W. Way	Second Assistant
10/06/1908–05/01/1909	James B. Hawkins	Second Assistant
10/10/1908–05/11/1907	Thomas J. Murray	Second Assistant
05/01/1909–05/?/1910	James B. Hawkins	First Assistant
05/18/1909–06/07/1909	K.M. Frost	Second Assistant
07/16/1909–10/?/1910	Francis G. Howe	Second Assistant
10/01/1909–07/?/1917	William F. Aichele	Keeper
05/22/1910–08/?/1910	Andrew Nelson	First Assistant
08/10/1910–?	Hans Christian Anderssen	First Assistant
08/27/1910–11/?/1911	George Doige	First Assistant

Dates	Name	Title
10/01/1910–11/?/1911	Randolph C. Howell	Second Assistant
11/21/1911–05/?/1912	Randolph C. Howell	First Assistant
12/05/1911–03/?/1912	George L. Costello	Second Assistant
03/16/1912–05/?/1912	William H. Wilcox	Second Assistant
05/06/1912–10/?/1913	Jesse Orton	First Assistant
05/06/1912–03/10/1913	Chester B. Harper	Second Assistant
03/10/13–11/16/1914	George J. Thomas	Second Assistant
10/03/1913–09/17/1914	Chester B. Harper	First Assistant
11/16/1914–03/27/1917	George J. Thomas	First Assistant
11/16/1914–07/13/1915	Herbert Greenwood	Second Assistant
08/20/1915–?	George F. Reid	Second Assistant
11/10/1916–03/09/1917	Edward A. Donahue	Second Assistant
03/20/1917–05/01/1920	Edward A. Donahue	First Assistant
07/?/1917–04/13/1919	George J. Thomas	Keeper
03/24/1919–04/21/1920	Charles Behounek	Second Assistant
04/30/1919–06/06/1921	Frank Oberley	Keeper
04/21/1920–06/23/1921	Charles Behounek	First Assistant
05/01/1920–08/07/1920	Marlin A. Postlewaite	Second Assistant
09/?/1920–?	Frank J. Conklin	Second Assistant
1921–10/30/1924	Norman B. Devine	First Assistant
04/04/1921–?	Edward W. Newton	Second Assistant
06/23/1921–03/?/1922	Charles Behounek	Keeper
07/16/1921–?/?/1922	William H. Bailey	Second Assistant
08/24/21–10/12/1922	Arthur Bessett	First Assistant
03/?/1922–11/07/1924	William H. Bailey	Keeper
03/09/1923–03/09/1923	Ralph E. Merithen	Second Assistant
08/?/1923–08/?/1923	John Ostman	First Assistant
10/07/1924–05/?/1926	Norman B. Devine	Keeper
11/21/1924–04/07/1925	Harvey H. Kenyon	Second Assistant

DATES	NAME	TITLE
1925–?	Stephen B. Holm	First Assistant
04/14/1925–?	Stephen B. Holm	Second Assistant
09/16/1925–07/?/1926	Isaac Karlin	First Assistant
11/04/1925–?	Hugo R. Carlson	Second Assistant
11/05/1925–?	Marvin O. Barrett	Second Assistant
07/?/1926–02/31/1928	Isaac Karlin	Keeper
1928–03/01/1929	James G. Spencer	First Assistant
01/03/1929–03/17/1930	James G. Spencer	Keeper
01/21/1929–04/01/1930	Frank Loftin	First Assistant
03/01/1929–04/01/1930	Arthur H. Miller	Second Assistant
04/01/1930–09/01/1930	Frank Loftin	Keeper
04/01/1930–1935	Arthur H. Miller	First Assistant
04/11/1930–?	Edward Sullivan	Second Assistant Keeper
08/02/1930–06/25/1934	Gilbert Burke	Keeper
06/25/1934–05/01/1941	Adrien J. Boisvert	Keeper
09/12/1934–10/01/1935	Gustav H. Axelson	Second Assistant
10/01/1935–05/17/1937	Gustav H. Axelson	First Assistant
10/01/1935–05/17/1937	Elmer F. O'Toole	Second Assistant
05/17/1936–10/04/1937	John A. Stockton	Second Assistant
05/17/1937–01/04/1937	Elmer F. O'Toole	First Assistant
10/04/1937–09/01/1938	John A. Stockton	First Assistant
10/04/1937–04/01/1938	Harry C. Buede	Second Assistant
09/01/1938–1943	Roy V. Wood	First Assistant

COAST GUARD RANKS BEGIN

05/?/1941–07/?/1943	Roy V. Wood	OIC
07/?/1943–11/18/1948	Shelbert Payne	OIC
04/09/1944–11/05/1944	Daniel C. Madden	?
07/01/1944–03/20/1945	Alois C. Fabian	BM1C
11/05/1944–1945	Fredrick S. Fennikok	S1C
03/12/1945–1945	Raymond C. Artin	?
1946–?	M.R. Vieira	BM2C
11/?/1946–11/?/1948	Frank Kuhne	BMC
05/19/1947–06/29/1951	Robert W. Hodges	BM2C
11/18/1948–12/21/1954	Gottfried Mahler	OIC
06/10/1955–10/08/1954	Robert W. Hodges	BM1C
12/25/1954–04/09/1956	George J. Barben	BT
03/?/1955–12/12/1959	Arnold A. Leiter	EM2C
12/?/1955–10/01/1958	Robert W. Hodges	OIC
04/15/1956–03/?/1957	Vernon G. Watts	EM3C
10/01/1958–03/30/1959	Edward H. Beck	OIC
04/15/1959–09/?/1959	Gene L. Michaels	OIC
12/15/1959–?	Richard A. Lee	EM
1963–?	Robert Fetters	?
11/?/1963–?	H.W. Lacroix	OIC
1965–1969	Duane Butler	?
12/?/1965–1969	Warren Kelly	?

Note: The above information was obtained from the Fire Island Lighthouse archives.

Abbreviations:
BMC: Chief boatswain's or bosun's mate
BM1C: Boatswain's or bosun's mate first class
EM1C: Electrician's mate or engineman first class
OIC: Officer in charge
S1C: Seaman first class

SPECIFICATIONS FOR THE 1826 LIGHTHOUSE

The Light House is to be an Octagonal Pyramid to be built of Connecticut River blue split stone and the best quick lime and sand mortar, the foundation wall to be seven feet thick from the base to the water table, and tapered to two feet six inches at the top of the pyramid; the height of the building to be seventy-four feet above the water table to the bottom of the lantern, thirty-two feet diameter at the water table, and sixteen feet diameter at the top of the pyramid; the foundation to be layers of square timber, thirty-four feet in length, placed transversely, six feet below the surface, and the water to be three feet above the surface; the water table to be of hewn stone, sloping at the top, a strong and substantial panelled door, three feet wide and lock thereon, hung upon strong hinges, well secured in the wall, in the first story, the flooring of which to be paved with large flat stone at the water table, the stories to be not more than nine feet, nor less than seven feet in the clear; the floorings to be supported with strong sound timber, and floored with one and a half inch plank, grooved together; the stairs to be of easy assent, and made substantially of plank and railed; six windows on the tower, three of which on the west, and three on the east side, with durable window frames and sashes, the sashes to be glazed with glass, 10 x 12 inches, of double thickness, four panes in each sash, and two sashes to the window; the doors and windows to have cut stone sills and lentils [sic]; the top of the tower to be arched over, leaving a scuttle on one side, of two feet three inches by three feet three inches in the clear; an iron frame around the same, and a door framed with iron and covered with copper, leaving also a well with an iron frame, about two feet square, which is to be left in all the flooring; to have a cut stone cornice of large stone, projecting over the top of the wall of the pyramid, on which wall and arch, a cut stone deck of four inches thick is to be laid and the stone secured together with iron clamps, the joints of stone and clamps to be filled in with lead; a complete iron lantern, octagon form, the posts of which to be of wrought iron, to be two and a half square, to run six feet into the stonework and to be there secured with eight large iron anchors; the lantern to be twelve feet diameter and the posts eight feet in height above the platform of the pyramid on which it is to rest; an iron plate to be framed on the top of the posts, and to be well braced and secured above with iron, the space between the posts at the angles to be occupied by the sashes which are to be of iron, molded on the inside, struck solid, and of sufficient strength, so as not to work with the wind; each sash to be glazed with white plate glass, ten by twelve inches, and one fifth of an inch in thickness; on the west side, part of the sash is to be hung and fitted as a door, to go out on the platform; the lantern to be surrounded by an iron balustrade, three feet high, each rail or rod to be an inch square, which is to be securely braced; the top of the lantern is to be a dome five feet high, water tight, and covered with copper, thirty two ounces to the square foot, formed by sixteen iron rafters, concentrated in an iron hoop at the top, which forms the funnel for the smoke to pass out of the lantern into the ventilator, made of copper in the form of a ball, sufficient to contain forty gallons, and large enough to secure the funnel against rain; the ventilator to be turned by a large vane, so that the hole for venting the smoke may always be to leeward; the lantern and ballustrade [sic] to be covered with three counts of black paint; the door, sashes, window frames, to be well painted with two coats of paint, and the building to be well pointed with cement, and white washed twice over, inside and outside, and furnished with two complete electrical rods, with points to each; and in every respect to be completely built with best materials and workmanship....A well to be sunk, of four feet diameter inside, of sufficient depth to procure good water, at a convenient distance from the house, to be stoned, and furnished with a curb, windlass, and iron chain, and a strong bucket and suitable house over the well. The Light House and dwelling to be completed by the first day of the December next. Separate proposals will be received for fitting the said Light House, within one month after it shall be built, with eighteen patent lamps and plated Reflectors, highly burnished, and all the necessary apparatus to make the same complete; the lights to be fitted up on the most approved revolving plan, eight double tin butts, with sheet iron covers of eighty gallons capacity each for keeping the oil. The whole to be approved by the Superintendent of the establishment, or such other person as may be designated by him.[102]

THE 1857 ITEMIZED ESTIMATE FOR THE COSTS OF BUILDING THE SECOND LIGHTHOUSE

800,000 bricks	$8,000
1,200 pounds of cement	$1,500
Stone for the foundation	$2,820
650 cubic yards of concrete for the foundation	$3,250
160 stone steps	$1,600
500 feet of stone for cornices	$500
Post iron	$1,000
Stone for floors	$300
Wrought iron ladders and railings	$200
Pay for 1,610 days of work by masons	$4,000
Pay for 250 days of work by carpenters	$500
Work by stone cutters	$375
Work by blacksmith	$300
Work by laborers	$2,500
Freight	$4,000
Machinery, tools, etc.	$1,500
Total	$32,345[103]

NOTES

Introduction

1. Perrault, *Fire Island Lighthouse*, 935.
2. Ibid., 942–43.

Chapter 1

3. Bang, *Fire Island*, 9.
4. Rattray, *Ship Ashore!*, 53–54, 202.
5. Wheeler, "Fire Island Lighthouse," 3.

Chapter 2

6. Perrault, *Fire Island Lighthouse*, 16; Müller, *Long Island's Lighthouses*, 287; Bang, *Fire Island*, 11–12.
7. Perrault, *Fire Island Lighthouse*, 16; Müller, *Long Island's Lighthouses*, 287; Bang, *Fire Island*, 11–12.
8. Wheeler, "Fire Island Lighthouse," 4.
9. Perrault, *Fire Island Lighthouse*, 17; Wheeler, "Fire Island Lighthouse," 4; Müller, *Long Island's Lighthouses*, 288; Bang, *Fire Island*, 12.
10. Müller, *Long Island's Lighthouses*, 289.

11. Ibid., 288–89.
12. Fire Island National Seashore archives.
13. Müller, *Long Island's Lighthouses*, 290–91; Bachand, *Northeast Lights*, 244.
14. Müller, *Long Island's Lighthouses*, 291–92.
15. Ibid., 292–93.
16. Johnson, *Fire Island*, 52.
17. Field, *Wrecks and Rescues*, 123; Dolan, *Brilliant Beacons*, 135–36; Bang, *Fire Island*, 12, 19; Perrault, *Fire Island Lighthouse*, 17; Wheeler, "Fire Island Lighthouse," 4; Müller, *Long Island's Lighthouses*, 288–89.
18. Rattray, *Ship Ashore!*, 9–10.
19. Field, *Wrecks and Rescues*, 123; Dolan, *Brilliant Beacons*, 135–36; Bang, *Fire Island*, 12, 19; Perrault, *Fire Island Lighthouse*, 17; Wheeler, "Fire Island Lighthouse," 4; Müller, *Long Island's Lighthouses*, 288–89.

Chapter 3

20. Perrault, *Fire Island Lighthouse*, 22; Field, *Wrecks and Rescues*, 1, 129; Bang, *Fire Island*, 13–14; *Fire Island Lighthouse–1858*, 3; fireislandlighthouse.com.

Chapter 4

21. Levitt, *Short Bright Flash*, 154–55, 163.
22. Ibid., 56, 58, 64, 83.
23. Ibid., 127, 129, 140–47; Perrault, *Fire Island Lighthouse*, 136.
24. Levitt, *Short Bright Flash*, 154–55, 163; Perrault, *Fire Island Lighthouse*, 17, 20.
25. Bang, *Fire Island*, 17–18; Perrault, *Fire Island Lighthouse*, 100, 104, 124.
26. Perrault, *Fire Island Lighthouse*, 17, 99, 101–3; Bang, *Fire Island*, 19.
27. Perrault, *Fire Island Lighthouse*, 104–6.
28. Ibid., 107–8; Müller, *Long Island's Lighthouses*, 296.
29. Perrault, *Fire Island Lighthouse*, 18, 326.
30. Ibid., 67, 319–20, 358, 523.
31. Ibid., 17.
32. Ibid., 102.
33. Bang, *Fire Island*, 9; Perrault, *Fire Island Lighthouse*, 138.

Chapter 5

34. *Fire Island Light Station Interpreter's Guide*, 37; Müller, *Long Island's Lighthouses*, 297–98; Tuomey, "Long Island's Famous."
35. *Correspondence Received*, 389; Perrault, *Fire Island Lighthouse*, 22.
36. Müller, *Long Island's Lighthouses*, 298.
37. Ibid.
38. Ibid., 298–99; Weston, "Finding the Beacon."
39. Perrault, *Fire Island Lighthouse*, 112.
40. Florence Schmalke, interview, transcript, Fire Island Lighthouse archives.
41. Aquaexplorers.com; Müller, *Long Island's Lighthouses*, 283.
42. Dolan, *Brilliant Beacons*, 359.
43. Perrault, *Fire Island Lighthouse*, 362.
44. Müller, *Long Island's Lighthouses*, 299–300.
45. Ibid., 300–1.
46. Perrault, *Fire Island Lighthouse*, 139–40.
47. Weissman, "Seashore Adds"; Fire Island Lighthouse Preservation Society, "Childhood Memories," 3–4.
48. Perrault, *Fire Island Lighthouse*, 22.

Chapter 6

49. Bachand, *Northeast Lights*, 12.
50. Müller, *Long Island's Lighthouses*, 301.
51. Ibid., 318–19; Bachand, *Northeast Lights*, 12.
52. Müller, *Long Island's Lighthouses*, 318–19.
53. Ibid.; Bachand, *Northeast Lights*, 13.
54. Bachand, *Northeast Lights*, 13; Müller, *Long Island's Lighthouses*, 318–19.
55. Müller, *Long Island's Lighthouses*, 319.
56. Ibid., 319–23; us-lighthouses.com; Bachand, *Northeast Lights*, 13; lighthousefriends.com.

Chapter 7

57. Perrault, *Fire Island Lighthouse*, 21, 141–42.
58. Bachand, *Northeast Lights*, 247; Müller, *Long Island's Lighthouses*, 302.
59. Perrault, *Fire Island Lighthouse*, 22.

60. *Brooklyn Daily Eagle*, "Advertising to Get a Wife Doesn't Pay, Lonely Man Finds," June 2, 1911; *Brooklyn Daily Eagle*, "Lighthouse Keeper's Advertisement Brought Him No Bride," July 1, 1911; *Brooklyn Daily Eagle*, "Hans Advertised for Wife; Now Happily Married," October 22, 1911; *Brooklyn Daily Eagle*, "Wife Won by 'Ad' Sues," January 25, 1912.

61. Müller, *Long Island's Lighthouses*, 301–2.

62. Ibid., 302.

63. Ibid., 301–2.

64. Ibid., 303.

65. Aquaexplorers.com.

66. Fire Island Lighthouse Preservation Society, "Childhood Memories."

67. U.S. Lighthouse Service, "Light Station Struck by Lightning."

68. Fire Island Lighthouse Preservation Society, "Childhood Memories."

69. Müller, *Long Island's Lighthouses*, 303.

70. Perrault, *Fire Island Lighthouse*, 940.

71. Weissman, "Seashore Adds."

72. Müller, *Long Island's Lighthouses*, 304; Perrault, *Fire Island Lighthouse*, 74, 22.

73. Perrault, *Fire Island Lighthouse*, 141–43, 312; Müller, *Long Island's Lighthouses*, 304.

74. Perrault, *Fire Island Lighthouse*, 523.

75. Emerick, "Boivert, Keeper of the Light"; Müller, *Long Island's Lighthouses*, 305.

76. Weather.gov; Müller, *Long Island's Lighthouses*, 305–6; Perrault, *Fire Island Lighthouse*, 525.

77. Müller, *Long Island's Lighthouses*, 309.

78. Ibid., 306–11; Mintz, "Keeping the Light Was Family Affair"; Kahlke, "Gottfried Mahler, Fire Island Lighthouse Keeper"; Olson, "Look Up, It's Santa."

79. Müller, *Long Island's Lighthouses*, 311.

80. Ibid., 312.

81. *Fire Island Light Station Interpreter's Guide*, 41.

82. Perrault, *Fire Island Lighthouse*, 163.

83. Ibid., 4, 144, 940; Bachand, *Northeast Lights*, 247; Müller, *Long Island's Lighthouses*, 302; U.S. Coast Guard, "Coast Guard Shifts Fire Island Light"; *Newsday*, "Turning Off a Landmark," March 18, 1972.

Chapter 8

84. Bleyer, "Work of Preservationists Shines."
85. Perrault, *Fire Island Lighthouse*, 940.
86. Ibid., 5.
87. Ibid., 9.
88. Ibid., 8, 533–37.
89. Mintz, "Fire Island's Beamin' Beacon."
90. Mintz, "$300,000 More Sought to Restore Lighthouse"; *Fire Island Light*, "The Final Stretch, the Tower Is Restored," November 1987; Fire Island Lighthouse Preservation Society, "Chronology of FILPS Involvement with Lighthouse."

Chapter 9

91. Fire Island Lighthouse Preservation Society, "Chronology of FILPS Involvement with Lighthouse."
92. Bleyer, "Fire Island Light in Loving Hands."
93. Bleyer, "Could Fire Island Lighthouse Lens Come Home?," 11.
94. Fire Island Lighthouse Preservation Society, "Chronology of FILPS Involvement with Lighthouse."
95. Bleyer, "Fire Island Lighthouse," 8.
96. Bleyer, "Fire Island Lens Back on Long Island," 9.
97. Fire Island Lighthouse Preservation Society, "Chronology of FILPS Involvement with Lighthouse."
98. Bleyer, "New Home for Fire Island Lens"; Bleyer, "Lens Returns to Fire Island Lighthouse."
99. Fire Island Lighthouse Preservation Society, "Chronology of FILPS Involvement with Lighthouse."
100. Ibid.

Appendices

101. Ibid.
102. Bang, *Fire Island*, 11–12.
103. Ibid., 18.

BIBLIOGRAPHY

Bachand, Robert. "Fire Island Lightship." *The Keeper's Log*, Summer 2000.

———. *Northeast Lights.* Norwalk, CT: Sea Sports Publications, 1989.

Bang, Henry R. *The Story of the Fire Island Light.* Fire Island, NY: Fire Island Lighthouse Preservation Society, 1988.

Bleyer, Bill. "At Fire Island, Seeing the Light." *Newsday*, February 22, 2006.

———. "Could Fire Island Lighthouse Lens Come Home?" *Long Island Boating World*, July 1999.

———. "Fire Island Lens Back on Long Island." *Long Island Boating World*, June 2007.

———. "Fire Island Lighthouse." *Long Island Boating World*, April 2006.

———. "Fire Island Light in Loving Hands." *Newsday*, December 19, 1996.

———. "Lens Returns to Fire Island Lighthouse." *Lighthouse Digest*, July–August 2011.

———. "New Home for Fire Island Lens." *Lighthouse Digest*, October 2010.

———. "Work of Preservationists Shines." *Newsday*, May 12, 1996.

Brooklyn Daily Eagle. "Advertising to Get a Wife Doesn't Pay, Lonely Man Finds." June 2, 1911.

———. "Hans Advertised for Wife; Now Happily Married." October 22, 1911.

———. "Lighthouse Keeper's Advertisement Brought Him No Bride." July 1, 1911.

———. "Wife Won by 'Ad' Sues." January 25, 1912.

Chang, Sophia. "Let There Be Lighthouse." *Newsday*, November 6, 2013.

Correspondence Received by Light-House Board, 1853–1900. National Archives, Letter Book No. 447.

Dolan, Eric Jay. *Brilliant Beacons: A History of the American Lighthouse.* New York: Liveright Publishing, 2016.

Emerick, Gertrude. "Boivert, Keeper of the Light." *New York Daily News,* January 20, 1935.

Field, Van R. *Wrecks and Rescues on Long Island.* East Patchogue, NY: Searles Graphics Inc., 1997.

Fire Island Lighthouse—1858. Patchogue, NY: Fire Island National Seashore, n.d.

Fire Island Lighthouse Preservation Society. "Childhood Memories of the Fire Island Lighthouse." *Fire Island Light,* November 1987.

———. "Chronology of FILPS Involvement with Lighthouse."

———. "The Final Stretch, the Tower Is Restored." *Fire Island Light,* November 1987.

Fire Island Light Station Interpreters' Guide. Fire Island, NY: Fire Island Lighthouse Preservation Society, 1995.

Gentile, Gary. *USS San Diego—The Last Armored Cruiser.* Philadelphia: Gary Gentile Productions, 1989.

Johnson, Madeleine C. *Fire Island, 1650s–1980s.* Mountainside, NJ: Shoreland Press, 1983.

Kahlke, Cheryl Dunbar. "Gottfried Mahler, Fire Island Lighthouse Keeper." *Fire Island Tide,* July 18, 2008.

Levitt, Theresa. *A Short Bright Flash: Augustin Fresnel and the Birth of the Modern Lighthouse.* New York: W.W. Norton & Company, 2013.

Mintz, Phil. "Fire Island's Beamin' Beacon." *Newsday,* May 26, 1986.

———. "Keeping the Light Was Family Affair." *Newsday,* May 26, 1986.

———. "$300,000 More Sought to Restore Lighthouse." *Newsday,* April 22, 1986.

Müller, Robert G. *Long Island's Lighthouses Past and Present.* Patchogue, NY: Long Island Chapter of the U.S. Lighthouse Society, 2004.

Newsday. "Turning Off a Landmark." March 18, 1972.

Olson, David. "Look Up, It's Santa!" *Newsday,* December 11, 2016.

Perrault, Carole L. *Fire Island Lighthouse and Keeper's Dwelling Historic Structure Report.* Lowell, MA: U.S. Department of the Interior, Northeast Cultural Resources Center, Northeast Region, National Park Service, 2004.

Rattray, Jeanette Edwards. *Ship Ashore! A Record of Maritime Disasters off Montauk and Eastern Long Island, 1640–1955.* New York: Coward-McCann Inc., 1955.

Tuomey, Douglas. "Long Island's Famous Beacon." *Long Island Forum*, November 1957.

U.S. Coast Guard. "Coast Guard Shifts Fire Island Light—Now at Robert Moses Park." News release, December 21, 1973.

U.S. Lighthouse Service. "Light Station Struck by Lightning." *Lighthouse Service Bulletin*, October 1, 1918.

Weissman, Richard. "Seashore Adds a 'Missing Link.'" *New York Times*, September 9, 1984.

Weston, Martin. "Finding the Beacon Burning in Her Past." *Newsday*, September 21, 1983.

Wheeler, Wayne. "Fire Island Lighthouse." *American Lighthouse*, Summer 2000.

Websites

aquaexplorers.com
fireislandlighthouse.com
lighthousefriends.com
us-lighthouses.com
weather.gov

INDEX

ABOUT THE AUTHOR

Bill Bleyer was a prize-winning staff writer for *Newsday*, the Long Island daily newspaper, for thirty-three years before retiring in 2014 to write books and freelance for magazines and *Newsday*. He is the author of *Sagamore Hill: Theodore Roosevelt's Summer White House* (The History Press, 2016) and coauthor of *Long Island and the Civil War* (The History Press, 2015). He contributed a chapter to the anthology *Harbor Voices: New York Harbor Tugs, Ferries, People, Places & More* published in 2008. And he was a contributor and editor of *Bayville*, a history of his Long Island community (Arcadia Publishing, 2009).

The Long Island native has written extensively about history for newspapers and magazines. In 1999–2000, he was one of four *Newsday* staff writers assigned full time to "Long Island: Our Story," a year-long daily history of Long Island that resulted in three books and filled hundreds of pages in the newspaper.

His articles have been published in *Naval History*, *Sea History*, *Lighthouse Digest*, *Civil War News* and numerous other magazines and in the *New York Times*, the *Chicago Sun-Times*, the *Toronto Star* and other newspapers.

Prior to joining *Newsday*, Bleyer worked for six years at the *Courier-News* in Bridgewater, New Jersey, as an editor and reporter. He began his career as editor of the *Oyster Bay Guardian* for a year.

Bleyer graduated Phi Beta Kappa with highest honors in economics from Hofstra University, where he has been an adjunct professor teaching journalism and economics. He earned a master's degree in urban studies at Queens College of the City University of New York.

CPSIA information can be obtained
at www.ICGtesting.com
Printed in the USA
LVHW072046031120
670577LV00006B/671

9 781625 859778